# MAKE FACEBC
# FOR YOUR BUSINESS

The complete guide
to marketing your business,
generating leads, finding
new customers and building
your brand on Facebook.

## Alex Stearn

This book is dedicated
to Sonia, Tony and Ollie.

# Any Questions?

Thank you for your recent purchase of 'Make Facebook Work for your Business' I really hope you have enjoyed the book and your business will benefit greatly.

If you have any questions about the book or about social media marketing in general, please do not hesitate to contact me by email at **alex@alexstearn.com** or on **Facebook at www.facebook.com/alexandrastearn** and I will do my best to reply as soon as possible. I also offer regular updates, ebooks and social media tips in my newsletter at www.alexstearn.com and a group on Facebook which is all about supporting each other in our social media efforts and networking. Would love you to join us at this link
http://bit.ly/yourgroup

Looking forward to seeing you in the group ッ

# Table of Contents

# WHY THIS BOOK?

SO YOU WANT to launch a Facebook marketing campaign for your business or maybe you've already done so and you're just not achieving the results you expected. Perhaps that's because you've found it difficult to build a sizeable following or your audience is simply not converting into paying customers.

Every day hundreds of businesses are setting out on their social media journey excited about the opportunities and possibilities that this relatively new type of marketing may be able to offer their business. Some are getting it right, reaping huge rewards, and managing to leverage the enormous power of the Internet through social media, but the majority are struggling to make it work at all. Those who are struggling often don't really understand exactly how social media works and launch into a campaign without any plan or strategy or without even knowing exactly what they are looking to achieve. They perhaps create a Facebook page and ask their web developer to add a 'like' or 'follow' button to their website, invite their friends and customers to join their page, and then start posting updates. After a while they realize that whatever they are doing is having little or no positive effect on their sales and they are left with the same questions:

- How do I leverage the almighty power of the Internet and Facebook to make money for my business?
- How do I find the people who are interested in my products?
- How do I draw these people away from Facebook and onto my website or blog?
- And the ultimate question, how do I convert all these people into

paying customers and actually profit from Facebook marketing? These businesses either continue to go round in circles waiting for a miracle to happen, give up altogether, or continue to believe that there is a way they can make social media work for their business and start looking for a solution to solve their problem.

This is exactly what I did and this is where my social media journey began. I started to look for a solution but kept coming up with the same brick walls, the same fluffy vague information about engagement, and lots of very expensive courses. I read books and blogs but they never really seemed to solve my problem and get to the heart of the matter.

I then decided to make it my mission to demystify the hype surrounding social media marketing and discover everything I possibly could about how to make all the major social media platforms work for any business. I studied literally hundreds of campaigns to see what was working and what wasn't and completely immersed myself in social media marketing until all my questions were answered. My aim was to discover how to utilize the almighty power of Facebook to help any business achieve their marketing goals. I made it my mission to leave no stone unturned in terms of a marketing opportunity which could help any business generate leads and ultimately increase their sales.

After 18 months of immersing myself in this subject, I am now delighted to hand this information over to you. My goal is to help you save your time and your resources and provide you with a highly effective system to make Facebook work for your business. In this book I am going to share with you everything you need to know to take your business to the next level and leverage the power of Facebook so you can achieve the highest profits, the best customers, the best ambassadors for your business, and make money 24/7.

This book is perfect for anyone who is seriously committed to growing their business and achieving incredible results. Whether you are just starting out or already up and running and uncertain how to make Facebook work for your business then this book is to going to teach you exactly how to do just that. You will have absolutely everything you need to learn, prepare, plan, and implement a campaign which is going to help you generate leads and find new customers.

The fact is, Facebook, and social media as a whole, is a game changer, a dream come true for any business and has completely revolutionized the way business is being done today. However, it is still just a marketing tool and while on the face of it seems free, if not used correctly and effectively, it is simply just a waste of your time and resources.

In this book you will not only learn the skills and strategies of Facebook marketing but also everything you need to know about how social media works in marketing and how to plan, prepare, and execute your campaign including:

- What social media marketing is, why it is so good, why it is absolutely essential for any business today, and why so many businesses are getting it wrong
- The psychology behind why people make buying decisions and how you can use this knowledge to succeed in your Facebook campaign and other social media campaigns as well
- The importance of defining your business, your brand, and your target audience and how to do this
- How to set clear goals and objectives for your social media campaign
- How to prepare your website or blog for success, capture leads, and build a highly targeted list of subscribers
- How to plan, create, maintain, and manage your Facebook campaign
- How to use the changes in Facebook's organic reach to your advantage
- Detailed information about how to set up your business profile

on Facebook

- The strategies you need to implement to attract the best prospects and build and maintain a targeted following on Facebook and build lasting relationships
- The importance of content and how to easily find ideas to create content for your page
- How to convert your followers into leads, paying customers, and ambassadors and brand advocates of your business
- How to constantly measure and monitor your campaign so you can steer your campaign to achieve your goals

A great deal of love and joy has gone into writing this book. Love of the subject itself and joy at the opportunity to share with you the information and knowledge within. I have devoted 18 months to researching and writing this book, along with the others in the series, in order to uncover the truth about social media. I truly hope you will be inspired and that your business will thrive and flourish by implementing the suggested strategies.

As mentioned above there are books available on Kindle and in paperback for each of the major social platforms including, Twitter, LinkedIn™ and SlideShare, Google+ YouTube, Instagram, Pinterest, and Tumblr, including the big book which covers the whole series and includes all 8 books. That book, Make Social Media Work for your Business, is available on Amazon for $9.99.

Even within the time it has taken to write this book, certain things have changed in the social media world and so some sections have been updated to reflect those changes. The world of social media is dynamic and therefore it is my commitment to keep updating this book as those changes occur. If you wish to keep up-to-date with latest social media updates, tips, and changes, please subscribe to my newsletter at www.alexstearn.com

# The Social Media Master Plan
# & Workbook
# Now FREE to download

The Social Media Planner and Workbook compliments this book and all the books in the series 'Make Social Media Work for your Business'. Once you have read the book I highly recommend that you complete this short workbook. It's designed to take you step by step through what you need to do to find your ideal customers, build your audience on social media and actually succeed to selling your products and services. It is not a substitute for reading the book but will help you apply your knowledge to your particular product or service. You can download your **Free** Ebook here:

## www.bit.ly/winsocial

# CHAPTER ONE

## *THE IMPORTANCE OF UNDERSTANDING SOCIAL MEDIA MARKETING*

BEFORE LAUNCHING INTO your Facebook marketing campaign, and so that you are absolutely committed when you do start, you will need to be convinced that social media marketing does actually work for businesses and that you are going to be able to make it work for yours. In this chapter, you will learn why social media marketing has gained so much attention, why so many brands are using it, and why it is so different from other forms of marketing. The aim here is to help you truly appreciate the power and importance of this relatively new method of marketing. Once you are totally convinced that the time you will be investing will be truly worthwhile, you will be ready to launch into your Facebook marketing campaign with strength, confidence, and conviction.

So what is social media exactly? Social media is the place where people connect with other people using the technology we have today. It's where people engage, share, cooperate, interact, learn, enjoy, and build relationships. The number of ways in which we connect with each other has grown massively in recent years from telephone, mobiles, email, text, video, newspaper, or radio to what we have today, the social media networks.

As humans, the majority of us want to belong, be accepted, loved, respected, and heard. We are social animals and social media has provided us with new tools which allow us to be more social, even if our lives are more hectic and we are living a long way from our friends and family. It's now not unusual for family and friends to be located at opposite sides of the country or even in a different country. Our lives have become far busier and more transient than ever, and yet we still crave the same social connections as we did 100 years ago when we would probably have been living in the same village or town as our family and friends.

The impact that social media is having on our lives and on businesses is massive. Social media has completely changed the way we communicate and the way we do everything. It has made connecting with people and building relationships so much easier. Now, staying in contact with someone we may only have met once is straightforward. We can find old friends we went to school or college with, and the opportunities for making new contacts are limitless. Social media has given us the ability to quickly and easily share ideas, experiences, and information on anything we like, and we can find out about anyone, any business, or anything. With the massive growth in smartphone ownership, most people can now access the internet instantly. We are living in a virtual world and we can literally connect to anyone, from anywhere, at anytime.

Understanding the reasons why people love social media so much will help give you a really good idea about how, as a business, you need to engage so you can connect,grow and maintain that your audience. Most people are on social media to be social, to connect with other family and friends, and to have fun. However, here are a few more reasons why so many use and love social media:

To be part of a community or common interest group
To express their feelings and have a voice
To reconnect with old college or school friends
To find out where their friends are
To tell their friends where they are
To announce a piece of news
To find out if a product or service is good

To connect with thought leaders

To make business contacts

To follow brands

To keep up-to-date with current affairs, football scores etc

To connect with famous people

To find inspiration and motivation

To learn by reading blogs, watching videos, and listening to podcasts

To help other people

To launch a business

To advertise and grow a business

To make new friends

To make new contacts

To connect with others in different countries

To make a difference

To be entertained

To communicate quickly and save time

To support important causes or people

To find a job

## The power and enormity of social media

Everyone is doing Social! Okay, so not everyone is, but the majority of people are! Wherever you go you will see somebody with their heads down looking at some device, and you can bet your bottom dollar that they are accessing some social site, whether it's Facebook, Twitter, Instagram, LinkedIn, YouTube, Google+, Pinterest, or Snapchat.

The growth in social media is huge, and it's no wonder that it is being called 'The Social Media Revolution.' Without going into too much statistical information, it's safe to say that your customer is probably using at least one social network, either for personal or business use, and they very likely accessing multiple sites.

All the social media platforms are growing at incredible speeds. You only have to type 'Social media statistics' into Google and you will blown away by figures in the millions and billions. Facebook now has over one billion users and 95% of those users access it at least once a day and some more than five times, a day More than one billion unique users visit YouTube per month, and Twitter has 215 monthly active users. The most popular websites are social. The world loves being on social.

## WHAT IS SOCIAL MEDIA MARKETING

Not long ago promoting a business could feel very much like being alone on a desert island. You could have a great idea but unless you had vast sums of money for television, magazine, or direct mail advertising then, frustratingly, your idea was very likely to remain a secret. Today it is totally different and social media has given businesses endless opportunities to reach their target audience, connect with new prospects, and enter new markets. The playing field has been leveled out, and now anyone with the right knowledge has more chance than ever of making their business a success.

Social media marketing is a relatively new form of marketing and refers to the processes, strategies, and tactics used by businesses on social networking sites and blogs to gain attention and ultimately increase their revenue. Businesses and large brands are now using the fact that people love to engage and connect with other people with the other important fact that they are very likely to find their target audience on social media so that they can do the following:

- Find, reach, and connect with potential customers
- Drive traffic to a website or blog
- Stay connected and communicate with existing customers. It is a well-known fact that existing customers are far more likely to purchase and also pay more for a product than someone who has not bought before.
- To build trust, interest, and loyalty by interacting with your followers (potential customers) so that ultimately they will purchase your product, continue to purchase your product, and hopefully recommend your product to their friends

- To produce content that users will share with their social network or recommend to their friends. Social media marketing strongly centers around the creation of content for a particular audience with the intention that it can be shared, 'liked', and commented on by the user. When this happens, the content is being passed to other users by word-of-mouth, the most powerful form of advertising.
- To listen and find out what your customers want

## THE BIG LINK, THE PSYCHOLOGY BEHIND BUYING BEHAVIOUR

Not only have successful marketeers recognized that people want to engage with people, they have also tapped into the psychology behind why people make buying decisions and incorporated this into their social media campaigns.

As a business you will need to understand a great deal about your customers in order to market your products successfully to your target audience. Understanding how and why people make the final purchase decision will go a long way to help you discern how to make social media marketing actually work for your business. There seem to be a number of common factors that influence consumers when they are making their buying decision. Leveraging and using this knowledge with your Facebook campaign will be incredibly powerful and a recipe for success.

### The 'like' factor

This is a biggie. When we look at the findings and the psychology behind buying decisions it often comes down to simply being likeable. Consumers are far more likely to buy a product from someone they like, respect, or trust. Word-of-mouth advertising has always proven to be the most powerful form of advertising and now Facebook has taken this to another level and managed to harness this online with the 'like' button. Having your business name or brand reach hundreds or even thousands of people is now possible, and someone only has to 'like' or interact with your business on social media and you can almost guarantee that someone else will see that interaction. The truth is people do business with people they like and are more inclined to spread the word to their network about deals and special offers from people they trust, and respect.

## Social proof

When a consumer finds themselves at a point of indecision they will look for social proof and seek advice and corroboration from others. They are far more likely to buy if they see that their friends or a similar group of people have bought or used the product. People generally seek advice or look to see what others are buying to get over their personal insecurity when making a buying decision. This is why you see so many women shopping in pairs. The opinion of a friend about an item can often be the deciding factor when making the decision to buy or not.

Facebook is one of the most trusted platforms when it comes to product or service recommendations. This is where the Facebook plug-ins come in. They actually display social proof by showing the faces of your friends or a number count of the people who 'liked' the product, article, or page. The reason this is so powerful with social media marketing is simply because seeing a large number of people 'liking' a product or service can be enough to persuade someone to make a buying decision, to read something, or to follow a business. The truth is that people trust the opinion of others more than they trust advertising, and in order to make social media marketing work, businesses need to leverage this fact.

## Authority and reviews

Even before the Internet was introduced, people were keen to find reviews about products they were interested in buying, particularly if they were planning to make a major purchase. They would either buy a special magazine or seek information from an authoritative figure on a TV advertisement. Today, however, shoppers are far more savvy. They can smell an ad a mile off and they will go out of their way to find honest reviews about something they may want to buy. They are also spoiledfor choice, not only with the number of products available to them but the fact that they can find a review about literally anything just by a simple search on the Internet or looking at a brand's Facebook page. People always have and always will want as much evidence as possible that they are making the right buying decision. Any business who wants to succeed today needs to embrace this fact and try and gain as many reviews for their products and services as possible. Reviews could be in the form of customer blog articles, reviews on your website, on social media sites, or articles in newspapers and magazines. Displaying articles, client testimonials, or the logos of magazines that you have been featured in on your website will also go a long way to building authority and gaining the trust of your prospects.

## Scarcity or exclusivity

Scarcity or exclusivity can play a big part in people's buying decisions, and Facebook is a perfect place to communicate and use this factor to sell your products. If a product is scarce or less available, the consumer will often perceive that this product has greater value. As it becomes less available, the consumer fears that they may lose out on a great deal or a one-time offer. Giving your prospects a deadline or a specific time to purchase something or redeem an offer is an incredibly powerful way of focusing their mind on making a decision. When they know they need to make that decision by a certain time or they may lose out on a one-time deal, they are far more likely to make that decision. Another very effective way of using this factor is by simply suggesting to your prospects that by signing up for your email opt-in, they will be the first to hear about your new products or your exclusive offers.

## Loyalty

Consumers do not like taking risks and often prefer to repeat their past purchasing behavior by buying from a brand they have bought from before. The majority of shoppers are brand loyal and social media is another way of nurturing this type of behavior by building up even deeper relationships with your customers through constant contact and updates.

## Reciprocation

Reciprocation is a very powerful factor to take into consideration if you are looking to succeed on Facebook. As humans, the majority of us have a natural desire to repay favors and with Facebook you can really put this into practice. By 'liking', sharing, or commenting on other people's content, you will attract their attention.. More often than not, they will return the favor by 'liking', commenting, and sharing your content. Also, if you are sharing great content on your network or offering good, valuable, and free advice, you are very likely to earn a great deal of respect. This will often result in a good payback of some sort later.

## WHY IS SOCIAL MEDIA MARKETING SO GOOD FOR YOUR BUSINESS?

We know that an enormous number of people are accessing the social networks to connect with each other and now we need to understand why this type of marketing is so different from other forms of marketing and why it is so important for your business. The main reason is that social media marketing is fundamentally more effective. Consumers today are smart, they are tired and suspicious of traditional forms of advertising, more often than not they will fast forward a TV commercial, switch channel or skip a printed page with an advertisement on it. Today's consumers want to hear that a product has been tried and tested, they want to see a product being demonstrated and they often need a recommendation from a trusted source to make a purchase, most probably a friend. Here are some reasons why social media marketing is more effective than other more traditional marketing methods:

## Social media offers you the opportunity to find the right target audience

Never before has it been so easy to find and access your target audience. With the information that Facebook and most of the social networks hold about their users you can now target and find the very people who are more likely to buy your products or services.

## Social media allows you to have a direct contact with your customer

Literally you have the opportunity to communicate directly and stay in touch with your customer, unlike traditional forms of advertising. For instance with a Facebook business page or a 'places' page you can stay in touch with your customers well after they have left your establishment or bought your product and you can send them offers to encourage them to return or buy again.

## Social media marketing harnesses the power of peer recommendation

The majority of people trust recommendations by others. Social media marketing is the only media that can harness the most powerful form of advertising, word of mouth, by making it possible for consumers to communicate with each other and vote for products or services by pressing the 'like' or 'follow' button.

## Helps builds your brand

Never has there been so much opportunity to build your brand. Your brand is simply the most valuable asset of your business. Your brand is what differentiates you from other businesses, it is the image people have of your business and it establishes loyalty. With social media you have the opportunity to engage with consumers and build positive brand associations in a way that no other media can. Consumers now have the choice and opportunity to follow your brand and if they do, this means they actually want to hear or see what you have to say.

## Humanises your brand

Social media allows you to communicate with your audience in a totally unique way. Your brand is no longer a rigid logo but a personality, not only can you show your appreciation and the value you place on your audience but they can also grow to love your brand too. No other type of marketing allows this type of two way live communication.

## Offers continual exposure to your product

Social media marketing allows you to be continually in contact with your followers. Once you built your audience they can hear from you and see your brand on a daily basis. Statistics prove that on average a person needs to see or connect with a brand seven times before purchasing. This is a difficult and costly goal to achieve with traditional forms of advertising but incredibly easy with social media marketing.

## The consumer has a choice

Unlike other traditional methods of advertising the consumer has the opportunity to be exposed to your product by choice, they can opt in or out whenever they want.

## Your audience is relaxed and receptive

The majority of people are accessing Facebook account and other social accounts to be social and in their own leisure time. Social media is all about connecting with friends and relatives, meeting new people and making new contacts. People are far more receptive to hearing from a brand in their own time when they are relaxed, as long as the brand is offering some kind of value is not continually pushing their product.

## You can continually engage with your audience

Social media marketing allows businesses to have an ongoing dialogue with your audience like no other media. Fans or followers who have interacted with a business on social media are far more likely to visit their online store than those who did not.

## It's viral

Once your followers choose to interact or share your content then this interaction is seen by their network of friends who are then also exposed to your brand. This is how viral growth happens which results in audience growth and brand awareness, more prospects, more customers and increased sales.

## Social media is an asset to your business

Unlike other forms of advertising where you see your marketing investment disappear your Facebook page or any other social account becomes a valuable asset. If you are using your social media marketing correctly your network will grow, you will be building trust and your asset will increase in value. With traditional advertising once an advert is delivered the connection with the buyer is over and you see your investment literally disappear.

## It is like having your own broadcasting channel

Once you have your campaign set up and your follower numbers are growing, you literally have your very own broadcasting channel which you own. You can communicate with your followers about anything 24/7. Nobody can take this away unless of course you are not running it correctly and you are losing followers. If you provide content that is so useful and interesting, your followers will keep coming back again and again to check if you have anything new to say. You then have a following of people who will associate your valuable content and their positive experience with your brand.

## You can offer your customers proof of trading

Having a social media presence which is active and engaging helps to reassure customers that your business actually exists. They can easily check, by comments left by customers, whether your business is reputable and trustworthy and they are far more likely to buy from you once they see your active presence on social media.

## Improve your search engine ranking

Google counts social sharing when ranking your website or blog. If people are finding your content valuable then the search engines will register this and rank your site accordingly. Social media sites are highly ranked in the search engines and having a well optimised profile is yet another way of being found on the internet.

## Opens up a worldwide playing field

It used to be only the large companies who could afford to build their brand and have the opportunity to access thousands of potential customers. Now everybody with a business has the opportunity to reach thousands of people both nationally and globally, grow their business and benefit from one of the most powerful forms of marketing. Having a business no longer needs be a lonely island, you literally have the opportunity to get your message heard by thousands of people through social networking.

## Provides advantages for the consumer

With just a few clicks of the mouse or the tap of a smart phone, consumers can be in contact with any business very quickly. For the first time they have a voice and a very powerful one, their opinions are taken seriously, they are and valued whether they are in contact through customer service or just following a brand because they are interested. People are wanting to remain close to the brands they are interested in and this is shown by the continual rise in the number of people following brands.

## You can listen to your customers

You can now hear what your customers are saying about your product or service and you can use this information to improve or develop your products and improve your customer service. This help your business to become more transparent and shows your customers that you care and value their opinion which ultimately leads to more trust for your brand.

## You can become a thought leader

By producing valuable and rich content for your audience you can become a thought leader. Not only will this help if you are a personal brand but will also helps to build trust and reputation for any business or brand.

## You can make a difference

With social media you can actually make a positive difference to people's lives. Once you know your audience you can provide content which is of value to them and which is actually going to help them in some way. Helping your audience like this goes a long way in helping them to remember your business when they are ready to make that purchasing decision.

## Endless opportunities

Never has there been so much opportunity to have direct access to so many people and neither has there been so much opportunity for any business of any size to have ongoing contact with so many of their potential customers. This is a marketeer or business owner's dream.

## IS SOCIAL MEDIA ACTUALLY WORKING FOR BUSINESS?

It is evident that the majority of major brands are running successful social media marketing campaigns. These brands are investing huge amounts of money, time and resources into this type of marketing, however you don't have to go too far to see whether social media marketing is actually working for business, simply ask yourself these questions:

- Would you prefer to buy a product if you knew that a friend or somebody you know of had tried it?

- Would you prefer to buy a product from a business or person that you do know rather than a business or person that you don't know?

- If you were thinking of buying a product from a business you had no history with, would you go and look to see if they had a social media site and see what other people were saying about their product?

If you answered yes to these questions then you can be pretty sure that social media marketing does actually work for businesses. It has to work doesn't it?

## WHY SO MANY BUSINESSES ARE GETTING IT WRONG

Even though most business owners have heard how powerful social media marketing can be, the majority are still unsure as to how to use it to benefit their business. So many Facebook pages have been created with enthusiasm only to be abandoned a couple of months, even weeks, down the line. Others are painstakingly posting consistently every day but posting the wrong type of content without a clue how to get their fans to buy their products. Many businesses are just paying lip service and seem to think that displaying a few social media icons on their site is enough to miraculously increase their revenue, and some are not even connected to any networks at all. Although on the face of it social media marketing seems free, it actually takes a sizeable investment of man hours, and if you are getting it wrong, you may as well be throwing a great deal of money out of the window. Here are some common reasons why so many businesses are getting it wrong:

### Not 100% committed and convinced

Many businesses are not convinced that it actually works at all and therefore are not prepared to put in the time it to learn how to plan and implement the effective strategies it takes to build a successful campaign. As a result, their campaign falls flat and they simply give up after a few months.

### Little or no understanding about how social media marketing works

Many still think that setting up a profile and putting an icon on their website is what it's all about. They may even post a few status updates and some pictures of their product in the hope that their website is suddenly going to be inundated with new traffic and that these new visitors are miraculously going to convert into customers.

## They don't understand the fact that fans and followers are worthless unless they know what to do with them

Just because a business has maybe 1000 or 30,000 fans or followers, it does not mean this will automatically transfer to their balance sheet. Fans are just fans, and as long a business doesn't know what do with those fans, they will stay as fans and not customers.

## Not understanding the psychology behind buying decisions

They have absolutely no idea about the psychology behind how and why people make buying decisions and, therefore, do not know how to use this knowledge to their advantage in their campaign.

## Lack of clear goals

Aimlessly sharing content on their network without setting specific and measurable goals is just a waste of time and resources.

## Not having a system to capture and convert leads

Building a following is almost useless if those followers are not visiting the business' website or subscribing to the newsletter so that they can be converted into paying customers. Many businesses are still not making lead capture one of their main goals.

## Unrealistic expectations

Social media is a long-term strategy. It needs to be an integral part of a business' marketing plan, and today, it's as important as any other daily task a business may undertake. It is not a one-size-fits-all solution nor a solution for overnight success. It takes careful planning and long-term commitment.

## The wrong audience

It's no good having a huge number of fans if they are not interested in buying your product. There are even sites where you can buy fans, but if they are not the right audience, they are very unlikely to be interested in what that business has to offer.

## Not enough followers

The majority of businesses are going to need a sizeable audience to make any impact at all. Although engagement is important, unless a business has a healthy number of followers, it's not going to be a great deal of benefit.

## Not being proactive

Many businesses seem to assume that people are just going to press the 'like' or 'follow' button on their blog or website. Unfortunately it doesn't work like that and people generally need a good reason or incentive to follow a business, unless it's a very well-known brand.

## Trying to push their products all the time

This is not what social media marketing is about. Businesses that continually push their products are just missing the whole point of how social media marketing works and will lose followers as a result.

## Posting too little, posting too often, or posting the wrong content altogether

If you post too much, your posts will be considered spam. If you post too little, you will just be forgotten. If you post the wrong content, you will not attract the right audience which may harm your brand. The top three reasons for losing fans are:

i.) The company posts too frequently

ii.) The business pushes their products too much

iii.) The business posts offensive content

## CHAPTER TWO

## *HOW TO RUN A SUCCESSFUL FACEBOOK MARKETING CAMPAIGN*

ONCE YOU HAVE made the decision to be 100% committed to your campaign, you fully understand the theory behind it, and you plan and implement the strategies and tactics outlined in this book your business is going to reap the benefits and you will in time develop an extremely valuable asset. One thing is for certain: if you choose to ignore social media, you can be sure that your competition will not and you'll be allowing them to steal the advantage. Social media is a powerful way to increase your revenue by driving sales, increasing customer loyalty, and building your brand while at the same time pushing down your cost of sales, marketing, customer service, and much more. Now let's get started!

So how do you leverage the power of social media and put it to work to benefit your business and produce amazing results? This chapter is designed to give you a brief overview about what is required to build a successful campaign so that as you read each chapter it will make more sense. Every aspect of this overview and everything you need to do and implement will be mapped out in more detail in the subsequent chapters.

The opportunity to reach an unlimited number of new contacts and prospects is available to every business today. You can safely say that your prospects are out there and all you need to do is know where to find them, how to connect with them, and how to capture and convert them into your customers.

Successful businesses are using Facebook and the other social media platforms in a totally different way from traditional methods of marketing. With Facebook marketing there is no need to employ pushy sales techniques. Once you put the essential work, planning, and system in place, you will find your products are practically selling themselves and your prospects are buying your products and becoming your brand advocates as a natural progression from your initial contact with them. The whole process is straightforward and as long as you carry out the necessary background work, planning, and preparation, you can make it work for your business.

## Know what you want

You need to have a very good idea where you want your business to be in the next one to three years. If you don't know what you want, then it is unlikely that your business will achieve anywhere near its potential. When you have a clear vision for your business, it helps you to focus and create the necessary goals you need to put into place to achieve that vision.

## Define your business, brand, and target audience

Brands establish customer loyalty, and Facebook offers you a huge opportunity to build your brand. In order to communicate in the right way, you need to create and consistently deliver the right message and brand experience to your prospects and customers. To do this, you need to define your business and define and understand your target audience so you can create your brand.

## Plan, plan, plan

Social media is not a quick fix. The majority of businesses start a campaign and then fall by the wayside. If you want to grow your business, then careful planning is required and it will involve creating your mission statement, setting clear and measurable goals and objectives, and planning your content strategy in line with who and what your target audience wants. Without a carefully crafted plan your campaign is extremely unlikely to reach its full potential.

## Prepare your business

Before launching your campaign you need to prepare your whole business so your brand and your brand message are evident throughout. You will need to communicate your brand through everything your do or say, including all your marketing material, brochures, promotional material, your website, your blog, and your email.

Your website is one of the best sales people you can have. It works 24/7 and can help to make your business turn up in your customer's home at the click of a mouse. When your prospect arrives on your website it immediately needs to make them feel that they have arrived at the right place, that you understand their needs, and that you can either provide a solution or give them exactly what they want. If you already have a website, you need to check that it has all the necessary features it takes to grab your visitors' attention, deliver the right message, capture them, and convert them into customers. Statistics prove that unless a business has a clever method of capturing leads, the majority of visitors to a website will leave without buying anything or ever returning again. Therefore, before even starting your Facebook campaign, you will need to check or create your website so that it does the job it is supposed to, which is to capture leads for later sales conversion.

## Set up your email campaign

Email is still one of the most effective methods of converting leads, and an up-to-date list of prospects who have given their permission for you to contact them on a regular basis has got to be one of your business' most valuable assets. Capturing email addresses on your website and through social media needs to be your most important marketing goal. Therefore, you will need to plan your opt-in campaign and set up an account with an email provider so you can continue to build a relationship with your prospects and sell your products.

## Create your Facebook page

Your Facebook page will, in many cases, be the first impression your prospects have about your business and it is as important as your website or blog. The aim of your page is to capture your prospects so that you can continue to communicate and build a relationship with them through their News Feed and through email. It is unlikely that the majority of your fans will return to your page after their initial visit so your page needs to grab their attention and make your prospects take action as soon as they arrive by 'liking' your page and joining your opt-in list. To turn your fans into customers you will need to install custom apps on your Facebook page. Depending on what type of business you have and what your goals are, you will need to determine what apps you to install. This could be anything from installing an app to capture email addresses to installing an app for a Facebook store.

## Create your Facebook posting calendar

Social media is not like traditional forms of advertising, so frequently pushing your products, posting ads, and plugging your business is not going to work and is likely to lose you fans. One of the most important things you are going to have to do for a successful Facebook campaign is to regularly produce and post compelling content that your audience actually wants to engage with and share. Facebook marketing is all about selling without selling, and the aim of producing content is not to directly sell your products but to do the following:

- Boost traffic to your blog or website, generate, capture, and nurture leads
- Create brand awareness
- Constantly remind your audience of your brand so when they are ready to buy, they buy from you
- Improve your ranking in the search engines
- Create engagement, build relationships, and encourage your audience to share your content with their friends
- Support others by 'liking', commenting on, and sharing their content

- Stand out as a thought leader and build your reputation as an expert in your industry

Create such good content that your audience stays 'liking' your page and continuing to read your updates, which builds and encourages brand loyalty.

Your content is where you can connect with your audience through their interests and passions. Your quality of content needs to be outstanding and you need to delight your audience with the best possible fresh, new, and compelling material. Excellence is what you should be aiming for with every update you make. The biggest thing to remember is that you need to tailor all your content to your audience's desires and needs.

Once you are absolutely clear about who your target audience is, what makes them tick, and what their values and aspirations are, you can determine what subjects and topics they will be interested in. The majority of the content you post will need to be about their needs and not yours. There is nothing more off putting and likely to lose you followers than continually posting about your business and shouting about your products or services. Of course you can do this occasionally if you have a new product or a special offer, but you need to be selective. Otherwise, your posts just become bad noise. Remember your followers are mostly on social media to be social. If your posts ruin their social experience, they will associate your brand with a bad experience and it won't be long before you start losing your fans and potential customers.

When you have decided on the subjects and topics you are going to create content about, you will need to create a Facebook posting calendar which will help you to consistently deliver this high-quality content. You will need to incorporate everything in this calendar, including any events you are planning, any special industry events, public holidays, blog posts, videos, and offers or contests you may be planning. You then need to map it all out so you know exactly how you are going to promote them on Facebook with the functionality you have available to do so.

## Build a sizeable and highly targeted following

The main aim of building your audience is to grow a community of followers who are interested in your products, will engage with your content, and become advocates for your brand. In order to have any impact at all you are going to need a sizeable number of targeted fans on Facebook. Building your audience will be an ongoing task, and it involves many different strategies which will be covered in this book. The size of audience and time it takes will depend on the time and resources you have available.

## The essential day-to-day activity

To build a strong presence, trust, relationships, and reputation, you will need to be active and nurture your fans. Social media is not a one-way street. It's an ongoing two-way communication. It's about going out and showing that you are interested in what others have to say, and it's about building community and getting your brand out there in the most positive light possible. Here are some of the things you will need to do on a day-to-day basis:

- Consistently post high-quality content
- Follow your followers and fans
- Engage, comment, share, and reply
- Show your audience you value and respect them
- Follow influencers in your niche
- Deal with negative comments

## Analyzing and measuring your campaign results

This book is all about how to make Facebook work for your business, and the only way you are going to find out if it is working or not is by constantly monitoring and analyzing your results. You will need to constantly check your results against the goals and objectives you have set. Once you know what is working and what is not then you can adjust and steer your campaign accordingly to achieve more positive results.

# CHAPTER THREE

## GETTING STARTED ON FACEBOOK

IT IS QUITE unlikely that any business today is going to limit itself to just one social media platform for marketing but there is one 'must have,' which is, of course, Facebook.

Facebook's mission is to give people the power to share and make the world more open and connected. Saying that Facebook has been successful in achieving their mission is an understatement. With over one billion users, Facebook is now the most popular social network and the largest referrer of traffic after Google. More time is spent on Facebook than any other social network.

Many businesses and most major brands now have a page on Facebook, and it's getting to the stage that not having a business presence on Facebook looks odd. Just seeing the number of fans and activity on the page will often be enough to reassure a prospective customer that the business is bona fide. It's now common practice for individuals to check to see if a business has an active Facebook page and see what other people are saying before purchasing.

Facebook offers endless marketing opportunities for both businesses and individual brands, and this book will offer you a comprehensive guide on how to harness the enormous power of Facebook to drive a successful marketing campaign and actually make Facebook work for your business.

This chapter will cover will cover getting started on Facebook, setting up your personal profile, creating your Facebook page, and getting it ready for business. To get started, here are a few basics about what a personal account is, what a Facebook page is, what a Facebook group is, and definitions of the terms that are commonly used on Facebook.

# THE BASICS

Each person who sets up a Facebook account is permitted to have just one account and one login. Personal timelines are for individuals to post status updates for their friends. They are not for commercial use and must be under the individual's name.

You are allowed up to 5000 friends on Facebook and if your goal is to share your personal status updates with a broader audience than just your friends, you can allow an unlimited number of people to follow you. Your followers will see your status updates that you post publicly in their News Feed. However, if your goal is to promote your business, under Facebook's terms and conditions, you will need to create a Facebook page.

## Facebook Pages

Facebook pages can be created by the official representative of a business, brand, organization , or celebrity. They are similar to personal timelines but unlike your personal profile, they are visible to everyone on the Internet and offer businesses. It gives you the chance to connect with a wider audience of Facebook users. Pages, therefore, offer numerous marketing opportunities for businesses to gain attention, build awareness of their brand, drive traffic to a website or blog, and ultimately increase sales.

Pages allow businesses to connect and share their content and updates with a fan base of customers and prospects who have voluntarily chosen to 'like' a page. People who 'like' a page will see the activity from that page in their News Feed. Businesses can then grow their target audience by either using Facebook advertising, encouraging their audience to share and engage with their content, and other marketing strategies.

Creating a page for your business allows you much more functionality than just having a follow button on your personal profile. They can be customized with the addition of apps, stores, events, and lots more, and they can be managed by the page creator. Admins have a profile on Facebook and have been appointed by the page owner.

## Facebook Groups

Facebook groups are where people can share their interests and opinions with others who have similar interests. Anyone can create a group around a common interest from their personal timeline. As with pages, group status updates will appear in the group members' News Feed, and they can share and comment with other members of that group. If a group is under 5000 members you can send updates to the group which will arrive in the members' Facebook mail.

Groups are more personal in nature than pages because the administrators have more control over who can join and participate and whether the group is publicly available or by invitation only. Groups are great for organizations , clubs, fan clubs, causes, church groups, and employee groups.

Facebook groups can have a number of administrators and be set up if you want more personal interaction, as the posts come from the administrators themselves rather than the page name since they are connected to the administrator's personal profile.

As a group, you have the ability to only let certain people join and you can set joining permissions. There are three types of groups:

- Closed - users need approval from an administrator of the group to join.
- Open - anyone can join.
- Secret - by invitation only. Businesses often use the Facebook group function to create a 'Secret Group' where only the group

members can see the posts. Secret groups offer a more private work and communication area and are ideal for coaching groups, groups set up to organize an event, or groups of people working together on an idea. Posts from group members will appear in the news feed of all the group members, everyone in the group can use the chat feature; documents and photos can be shared among members.

You may want to create a group to build awareness around a certain product, but you need to think carefully about whether you have the time to manage both a group and a page. Joining a group which is already running may be a better option for you. This will obviously depend on the resources you have available.

## YOUR FACEBOOK DICTIONARY

Just in case you are unfamiliar with Facebook terminology, here are the common Facebook Terms and their definitions:

**Timeline:** Your timeline or profile shows a history of all your status updates, photos and videos, and anything you have posted.

**News Feed:** This is where you see all the status updates of your friends, people you follow, and pages you have liked.

**Cover Photo:** This is the large picture that spans the space at the top of your page.

**Profile Photo: This** is the small box at the top left of your profile where you can display your photo or maybe a logo on your page.

**Friend:** A connection on your personal profile is called a friend.

**Friend request: This is** a request you send to another user, or they send to you, so you can connect and view each other's status updates.

**Status Update:** This is anything you post in the status update box. This could be an image, text, video, or podcast.

**Like: This is** the action taken that shows your approval of an update from one of your friends or an update from a page you have liked.

**Comment:** Users can leave a comment in the comment section of any status update from a friend or page they have liked.

**Share:** If you see an update that you like and you want your friends to see this update you can share it on your timeline by pressing the 'share' button. This includes anything from within Facebook and outside of Facebook on external websites which are accompanied by the share button.

**Message:** A message is a private message that you can send another Facebook user.

**Poke:** The poke is a gesture on Facebook used to get someone's attention.

**Pages:** Facebook pages are for businesses, organizations , celebrities, and bands.

**Privacy settings:** Privacy settings let users control who can see their posts.

**Tagging/Tags:** Users can tag other users in posts and photos. When someone is tagged, the post will appear in their timeline.

**Reach: This is** the number of people who see a status update.

**Admin: This is** a user who is given access to a business page and can make changes to it.

**Chat: This is** the instant messaging service that is available to all users on their personal profile.

**The Ticker:** The ticker is a column on the right side of your News Feed that lets you see things as they happen on Facebook in real time. If you have the subscribers' button activated on your personal profile, your public notifications will appear in the ticker of your subscribers. You can interact with any item on the ticker by hovering over any item. Every time you add a picture to either your personal profile or your business page it will appear in the ticker. Also, any comment that has been made on any post will appear in the ticker. Basically, the ticker lets you see things as they happen.

## SETTING UP YOUR PERSONAL PROFILE

The first thing you need to do if you have not already done so is to set up your Facebook account. This is very straightforward and once you have created your personal profile, you will be able to create your business page or a Facebook group. If you do not already have a personal profile on Facebook you will be offered the option to create a page for a celebrity, band, or business. Do not be tempted to click this or you will set up a business account which is quite different from a Facebook page which is attached to a personal profile. A business account does not offer you the marketing opportunities that a page offers and you cannot have a personal profile and a business profile under the Facebook terms and conditions. Basically if you choose a business account over a personal profile you will be unable to utilize certain aspects of Facebook such as:

- You will have limited functionality.
- You will not be found in 'search.'
- You cannot send or receive friend requests because you will not have a personal profile.
- You cannot build apps.
- You can only build one Facebook page.

**NB** If you do already have a personal profile and you want to use this for business, you can convert this into a business page. However, all in our slightly this is not recommended for the reasons above. It's always best to have a personal profile and then create a page for your business, and when you are completing your personal profile you will need to use your own name and not your business name. Facebook terms and conditions state that Facebook timelines are for personal use only and not commercial and they must represent an individual and be held under an individual's name.

## Personal profile photo and cover photo

Many businesses use a business logo on their Facebook personal profile as they feel it is a good way to get their brand out there when they are commenting on other people's posts. However, people see through this and are put off because they see this as an individual pushing their business and not really connecting and trying to build relationships. People like to connect with people and not logos. The place for a business logo is on your Facebook page. Your personal profile photo should contain a professional and friendly looking head shot of yourself and it needs to be 180 X 180 pixels or more and Facebook will shrink your image automatically to 160 X 160 pixels. You can get really creative with the image for your cover photo and you can definitely use this to show who you are in your personal and business life if you wish. Your cover photo image needs to be 851 X 315 pixels.

## Promoting your business on your personal profile

When you complete your profile information you will be asked for where you have worked. This is where you will be able to display your business page name once you have created it. If you do not want to publicize the fact that you have a business page then you can leave this blank and remain anonymous as far as your business is concerned. However, if you are planning to network, displaying your page name on your profile will be much more advantageous than if you don't display it. When you go and 'like' or comment on another page from your personal profile, the people who check back to see who you are will be able see you have a business. When anyone hovers over your page name they will be able to view a mini shot of your business page and can 'like' your page from there or send you a message.

When it comes to adding your contact information, you will find a space where you can add the link to your website or blog. When you have fully completed your Facebook profile, you can use the friend finder to start connecting with your friends and then you can start posting your status updates.

**Adding the 'Follow' button to your profile**

If you want to share your posts on your personal profile with more than just your friends you can do this by adding the **Follow** button to your profile. This is similar to the Twitter **Follow** button. Doing this allows you to share your posts with your subscribers as long as you have set your post to **Public**. There are advantages to doing this, particularly if you are a personal brand. It can be a much more personal way of connecting as people do like to connect with people. However, this Follower option does not offer you the marketing opportunities and analytics that a business page does so it may be a good idea to have Followers and also create a business page. This way you can invite your subscribers along with your friends to like your business page. To add the **Follow** button simply go to your settings page, click on **Followers** on the right hand side, and select **Everybody** from the drop down menu.

**Controlling your privacy on your personal profile**

Once you have set up your **Subscribe** button, you will probably want to make sure that your content is reaching the right people and that you are keeping the posts you want to have only your friends see marked as personal. You need to make sure that your privacy settings on things like photo albums are set to **friends** and not **public.** To make sure that your contact information is not viewed by the public, simply click on **Edit Profile** and then **Contact Info** and then choose **Friends** in the drop down menu.

**Things you can do with a personal page and not a business page**

Before going on to creating your Facebook page there are a number of things that you should know about what you can do on your personal profile but not on your page, these include: wishing your friends a happy birthday, sending private messages, and all the following:

- **Participating in groups:** Participating, commenting, and posting in groups are a great way to network, but they can only be done from your personal profile.

- **Subscribe to and comment on personal profiles:** If the individual has allowed subscribers to comment on their status updates, you can do this from your personal profile. This is a great way of making new connections and starting to building relationships.

- **Create interest lists:** When you create an interest list of individuals or pages from your personal profile, your list is available for public view. You can add yourself to a list, if the subject is relevant, which gives you the opportunity to be followed by the subscribers of that list.

- **Suggest your page to your friends:** You can only invite your friends to like your Page from your personal profile.

- **Chat:** You can only use chat with your friends on your personal profile.

## FACEBOOK LISTS

Facebook lists are available on your personal profile and help you organize the people you connect with and the things that you are interested in. They let you control who you post your content to and also let you choose whose content you see.

Just before you post your status update you can choose from the drop down menu next to the word **post** and select who you want to post to. It may be that you want only close friends to see certain posts or maybe just family or maybe do not mind everyone seeing it and therefore you can choose public. You can have lists for close friends, acquaintances and family and you can even put people who you do not want to see your posts on the restricted list. You will see all your lists on the left hand menu under **Friends**.

## Smart Lists

Facebook also compiles what are called **Smart lists** which are lists based on your interests or things you may have in common with your friends, for example, school, college, work or maybe the area that you live in, etc. To see your smart lists simply click on **Friends** in the left hand side of your news feed. You can edit these lists if you like simply by clicking on the list name and then Clicking on **Manage List** on the top left of the page.

## Custom Lists

Custom lists are lists you can create yourself and these are particularly good if you have potential customers mixed in with your friends. If you click on **More** next to **Friends** on the left of your news feed your lists appear here and then you can click **Create List** on the top right. You can name your lists whatever you like as nobody else will see this list. Custom lists allow you to post only to people you want to and also manage updates in your news feed. Here is how you do that:

- **Posting to custom lists** When you go to make a status update you can then select who you want to post to on the drop down menu beside the blue **Post** button.
- **Managing your news feed** Custom lists let you view only the updates you want to view. You simply select the list you want to see on the left and Facebook filters those particular posts for you . You can also add a list to your favourites by hovering your mouse over the list name and clicking on the pencil icon.

## Interest lists

Interest lists let you add people you are subscribed to and also pages that you like, as well as your friends. This helps you to keep up to date with those who you are really interested in. You will never see every single post with Facebook Edgerank (an algorithm that Facebook uses to determine what appears in the News feed) so creating an interest list helps you to makes sure you see everything you want too see and you are not missing anything from those pages you are particularly interested in. You can also share your interest lists with everyone on Facebook.

To create an interest list simply go to www.facebook.com/addlist You can select from pages you have liked and people you have subscribed to . You can then name your list and choose who can view that list: public, friends or only you. **Top tip:** make sure to add yourself and your page to the list!

Facebook offers you suggestions of lists that you can follow which is a great way of finding pages you may be interested in.

## CHAPTER FOUR

## *CREATING AND BUILDING YOUR FACEBOOK PAGE FOR SUCCESS*

IN THIS CHAPTER you will learn how you can maximize on the marketing opportunities available to you by creating a Facebook page for your business. You will learn how to best create and prepare your page so you are ready to start promoting your brand, building your audience, posting content, and converting your audience into customers.

Your page is going to be the central focus to grow your business on Facebook and is as important as your website as a source of traffic. This is where you are going to welcome your customers, introduce your business and brand to your future customers, and continue to connect with them on a daily basis. This is also where people will be going to check to see if you are a genuine and active business. In many cases your page will be the first impression your prospects receive about your business. Your page is going to be a dynamic hub of activity. It's going to be where you engage and build relationships with your target audience and it needs to scream out your brand in your page name, business description, profile picture, and cover photo.

## *GETTING YOUR PAGE READY*

To create your Facebook Page you need to be the official representative of an organization, business, brand, or public figure. To set up your page, go to the bottom of your personal profile page and click on **Create a Page**. You will then need to select your type of business, whether it is local, company, brand or product, or artist. It is very important that you choose an accurate category for your business as it is prominently displayed alongside your profile photo. When finished, agree to the terms and conditions.

If you have a business where you actually have a physical location then the **Local Business or Place** option allows you to take advantage of Facebook's location feature and you can enter your location details here. You will then have what is called a Places Page. There are details at the end of this section about Places Pages and how to claim it if it has already been taken.

Facebook will take you through a process of setting up your page, including adding your business name, website URL, a description of your business, and profile picture. You will then be offered the opportunity to invite contacts and friends, however, it's best to skip this section until your page is properly set up. After you have agreed and ticked the terms and conditions box, your page will be public. You can change the visibility of your page until it is fully set up by simply clicking **Settings** and then check the box **Unpublish Page** under **Page Visibility**. You can view and edit everything you have entered about your page including your business type. Simply click **Settings** on the top of your page and then **Page Info.**

Once you have set up your page, this will be completely separate from your personal profile. The fans of your page will not be able to see that you are the owner of the page unless you have publicly listed yourself as admin for that page. Also, your friends will not be able to see who the owner of your page is unless you decide to add it to your 'Work and education' section on your personal profile.

**Information for local businesses, claiming your places page, and the nearby places tab**
There are many advantages to having this type of page, particularly with the **nearby places tab** for mobile which allows Facebook users to see

which establishments are nearby to them at any time. With the nearby tab you can:

- Find a business and find directions
- Check in when you arrive
- See which of your friends have visited previously
- Like the business
- Recommend the business
- Share with your friends
- Call the business

When creating your page it is really important to complete all the sections about your location so you maximize the opportunity for your business to be found. With the introduction of Facebook's graph search it is likely that businesses which have the highest number of check-ins and recommendations will be ranked higher in a Facebook search.

### Claiming your places page

Your places page may have been created if someone has already visited your business and checked in and a new places page will have been created to represent that location. You can claim your page by simply clicking on the 'gear' icon and then selecting **Is this your business?** Here you can add information about your business and verify your business by either email or other documentation. If you find that someone else is managing your places page, simply click on the 'gear' icon of that page and select **Report Page**.

### Naming your Page

Your page name is what is going to appear in your fans' news feed every time you post or make a comment. It's incredibly important to get this right from the very beginning as once you reach 200 fans it cannot be changed. You need to use your business name or a name that truly represents your brand. You may find it advantageous to use your business name together with your own name, as people like to connect with people.

It may be tempting to cram your page name with lots of generic keywords to get found in a search, but this is not a good idea since people are unlikely to 'like' or share pages which look impersonal. There are lots of opportunities for adding searchable generic keywords in your description and **about** section. It is also important not to choose a generic term as in Facebook's terms it states that page names must not consist solely of generic terms. Facebook is cracking down on this and they have actually blocked publishing rights for some pages due to a violation of their terms and conditions. You are also not allowed to use or include unusual capitalizations, character symbols, numbers, professional titles, and trademark designations.

Another thing to consider is that even though you have up to 75 characters for your page name, it may be important to keep it shorter, particularly if you are going to advertise, as the Facebook ad titles only allow a maximum of 25 characters.

## Uploading your profile photo

Your profile photo can be either your logo or a photo of yourself, depending on what you are promoting. This image is embedded in the cover photo so both these images need to complement each other. If you are a personal brand, a photo of yourself is often a better choice rather than a corporate logo as people tend to connect much better with faces than logos. It's worth spending time to take a really good head shot of yourself in well-lit surroundings. Once you have this you can use it on all your social platforms to keep your brand recognizable and consistent.

Whichever image you decide upon needs to be at least 180 X 180 pixels. and it will be automatically cropped and displayed at 160 X 160 pixels. If the image is smaller than this, it will be stretched to fit the space which will not look good. Once added, you can click on your image and add a description and URL

## The cover photo area

Your cover photo is the most valuable area of marketing real estate on your page. This is where you can really shout-out and promote your brand and use this space to communicate, visually, exactly what your business is about and how you can help your ideal customer. Many businesses miss out on this opportunity by just uploading a fairly generic image without any message and the visitor is left feeling they have no real reason to press the 'like' button. This is not what you want. When it comes to your cover photo you have two main goals:

### 1. To get your visitor to 'like' your page

The action of liking a page is important not only because you get to stay in touch with your fans but also the action of liking your page is very likely to be seen in the news feed of your fan's friends. This word-of-mouth advertising is one of the most powerful forms of advertising.

In many cases, the first time your visitor arrives at your page may often be the only time they actually see your page in its entirety. After that, they may not have a reason to actually return to the page itself. It is therefore of paramount importance that whatever you put on your cover photo impacts your ideal customer enough to get them to 'like' your page. In order to do this, you need to grab their attention by choosing a compelling image and creating a message that connects with them emotionally. Your message needs to let them know immediately that they have arrived at the right place by stating clearly how you are going to help them or offer them a solution to their problem. The right image and message is a winning combination. If you are targeting the right audience, they are very likely to press the 'like' button.

### 2. To get your visitor to sign up to your email opt-in

One of the most important things to realize with any social media profile is that you don't actually own it. Changes are taking place all the time and although social media is incredibly powerful, there is nothing more important than building your own list of ideal customers. Your next goal is therefore to get your visitors to opt-in to your email list. This way, you have permission to communicate with them on a regular basis through their email inbox. You can do this in two ways: you can either send them to another page within Facebook using a custom application (instructions about how to do this later) or send them to a separate landing page off Facebook where you can collect their email address.

## Using your cover photo to collect leads within Facebook

You can use your cover photo to direct your visitors or fans to a custom page within Facebook which houses a form where you can collect their name and email address or any other information you require.

Custom pages are created by using custom applications which allow you to add virtually any type of page to promote your business or products. These pages can also be used for a competition, an email sign-up page, a sign-up for a webinar, or contest. To create custom pages you will either need to find a web developer who can set up an application or you can use one of the many websites on the Internet, like www.heyo.com, www.shortstack.com, or www.grosocial.com, who create custom applications. Some email service providers like www.constantcontact.com and www.mailchimp.com also provide apps for social campaigns like this.

By adding the details of your offer on your cover photo with a clear call-to-action and an image of an arrow, you can direct your visitor to any page within Facebook using any of the call-to-action buttons which are available within your cover photo.

## Using your cover photo to collect leads outside Facebook

The other effective way of collecting leads is to send your fans or visitors to a page on your website where you have a compelling offer and a form to capture their name and email address. You can use your cover photo to promote your offer by adding the details of your offer to your cover photo and then using any of the call-to-action buttons to direct your visitors to any URL you choose. This could be your website or blog or a specific landing page for a particular offer. Companies like www.leadpages.com or www.Instapage.com let you create landing pages for lead capture using any of their templates, and you can also publish these pages to a custom tab on Facebook.

**Facebook call-to-action feature**

Facebook have been rolling the call-to-action buttons since December 2014. By now most businesses will have had the opportunity to add a call-to-action button to their Facebook page.

There are seven call-to-action buttons to choose from;

**Book Now** (Book appointments, tables, or hotel rooms)

**Contact Us** (To help customers find your local business or contact you)

**Shop Now** (Drives people straight where you sell your products)

**Sign Up** (Very effective if you want to grow your email list)

**Watch Video**

**Use App**

**Play Game**

These buttons are great for a few reasons:

- **Calls to action work:** A call-to-action is the most effective tactic to convert random traffic into loyal customers

- **To set clear goals:** These buttons have given business owners the clarity they need to actually decide what goals they want to focus on for their Facebook page. Up until now there has been a certain vagueness about Facebook pages for businesses, but now these buttons are the icing on the cake and have made it even easier for the Facebook page visitor or 'liker' to take action and the owner to benefit from this action.

- **To Measure Results:** Now businesses can measure the success of their page with the metrics provided by Facebook. These statistics are great for testing because they let you see how effective each call-to-action is. For instance, you could try and test the various calls-to-action one week at a time to see which one is the most effective. You never know. You may be surprised.

- **How to add your call-to-action button to your Facebook Page** Adding your call-to-action is incredibly simple. You click on the call-to-action button on your cover photo and then click 'Edit call-to-action' from the drop down list. It will offer you seven options to choose from and then you simply add the URL where you want your visitor to go to. If you want to make it more obvious then you can add an arrow to your cover photo to help draw attention to the button.

## Designing your cover photo

To make your photo stand out and look as professional as possible it's important to keep it as clean and crisp by using a strong, colorful, and bold image. When you add text it's important to keep it to a minimum so you can make the message you want to deliver as clear as possible. Since Facebook lifted their rules governing what you are allowed to put on your cover photo, this area is even more valuable. You can now add your website URL, email address, pricing information, contact information, and a call to action.

There are many inventive ideas for cover photos. Just by browsing other Facebook pages you can find inspiration, and there are also many custom tools available on the internet for creating cover photos, like www.pagemodo.com . Using a graphic designer to create your image may be a good idea, and they can size it to fit all your other social profiles as well. The dimensions of the image you need for Facebook are 315 X 851. Once you have added your image you can reposition it and then if you click the image, you can add a description and URL.

You can change your cover photo whenever you wish. You could do this for a special offer which ties in with a special occasion, season, or holiday. Not only will your new fans see this when they arrive on your page but also your existing fans will see your new photo in their news feed as well, which is a great way of reminding them about your brand.

## Your business descriptions

With the introduction of Facebook's graph search, never has there been a more important time to make sure you complete all the written descriptive sections on your page and make the most of every bit of space available. All Facebook pages are indexed by Google, but with the new graph search, it is even more vital for you to be found within Facebook by as many keywords relating to your niche as possible. You can edit all your descriptions by clicking **Settings** and then **Page Info.**

## The About section

The 'About' section of your page can be viewed by clicking **About** under your cover photo and also on the left side of your page. Depending on the type of business you are, Facebook will pull in different types of information into your 'about' section. If you are a 'Places page' then details of your address, telephone number, opening hours, and type of business are going to be displayed here.

With other types of businesses, the 'About' information is pulled in from the short description. The information you offer about your business needs to be concise and thoughtfully put together so your audience knows exactly what your business is about after reading the first sentence. In your short description you need to include a brief summary of what your business is, how it will benefit your fans, and include your website URL. You can expand on your business in more detail in your long description. The more relevant keyword rich and search engine friendly information you include the better, but most importantly you need to make it interesting reading for your audience.

## Start date

The start date does not need to be the start date of the page but can be the start date of your business. A great way of adding interest to your page is by giving a brief history or the story about your business by adding events or milestones which have already passed. You can do this as long as you have created your start date sometime in the past.

## Choosing a vanity URL for your Facebook page

When you have created your page, Facebook will automatically assign a URL with a number. However you can change this to something more memorable like facebook.com/yourbusinessname, which will be much easier to direct people to. To change it you will need to have 25 fans on your page then you can choose your vanity URL or Facebook username. To create your vanity URL simply go to your 'About' page where you can change your **Facebook web address.** It is best practice to use your business name or, if that is not available, then something that is going to be easy to remember. After you have set your username you may change it only once. If your trademark name has been taken, you can notify Facebook about retrieving it.

## Your message settings

You can choose whether or not users can send you a message on your Facebook page. If you do choose to allow users to send you messages then this will be clearly displayed on your Facebook page with a message box below your cover photo. To change whether you want to allow people to send you messages, click on **Settings** and then **General** and you can edit your **message** settings there.

It is definitely advisable to allow your fans to send you messages. If you do not, then you are cutting off possible communication, turning away opportunities to connect, and making your business look cold and unwelcoming.

## Admin roles

If you are going to have a team of people managing your Facebook page you can set up admin roles. Facebook allows you to set up unlimited admin roles. As manager you can assign different levels of access depending on what each person is allowed to do.

To find this section simply click on **Settings** and then **Page Roles.** There are 5 admin roles: Manager, Content Creator, Moderator, Advertiser, and Insights Analyst. Each role has different permissions so you can control what each person is allowed to do as follows:

- **Admin** can manage admin roles, send messages, create posts on the page, create ads, and view insights.
- **Editor** can edit the page, send messages, create posts on the page, create ads, and view insights.
- **Moderator** can respond to and delete comments on the page, send messages on the page, create ads, and view insights.
- **Advertiser** can create ads and view insights.
- **Analyst** can see who created or commented on a post and can view insights.

## CUSTOMIZING YOUR PAGE WITH APPS

Facebook allows you to customize your Facebook page. By using custom applications, you can add promotions, contests, stores, email sign-up pages, videos, and more. Once you have added your custom applications they can be viewed by your fans in two places: below your cover photo and on the left sidebar of your page. Below your cover photo you can display up to two tabs, and the rest will be listed under the **More** tab. Creating a really interesting and unique page is what is going to make your page stand out from the crowd. There are four apps which have been developed by Facebook. You will see **Photos** under your cover photo and the other three ( **Video**, **Notes**, and **Events**) can be found by clicking **Settings** and then **Apps**.

### Photos

The photos app is where all the photos are displayed and can be organized into albums. When you add a photo you have the opportunity to add a description and a URL, so if you are adding products, you can direct the user to the page where they can buy that product. It is extremely important to complete all details and optimize your photos so you can maximize the chance of being found in a search.

## Events

Facebook can be a powerful platform for marketing any event, party, product launch, or trade show. The events app lets you create an event from your personal profile or business profile. This will be covered in depth later.

## Notes

The notes app offers you your very own built-in blogging platform. Even if you have your own blog, it's a really good idea to copy your blog posts into the notes. Notes are incredibly underutilized by Facebook users, but they are incredibly straightforward to use and another way of getting found within Facebook. You can add a title, upload a photo, tag people's pages, and there is basic formatting available too. When you create a note it will appear in your News Feed, and that of your fans, with an image if you have added one.

You can also use an app to automatically syndicate your blog posts to Facebook and Twitter with an app called NetworkedBlogs, which works through your Facebook account. To do this, simply type "NetworkedBlogs" into Facebook search and add the app, register your blog, and then go through the steps to pull your blog into Facebook.

## Video App

To use this you will need to actually upload videos directly to the Facebook video app. Facebook offers you the opportunity to upload a video directly from your webcam, which is great if you have updates you wish to post quickly.

## Displaying and viewing your apps

You can display two custom apps under your cover photo and if you wish to add more apps, they will be displayed by clicking **More** under the cover photo and also on tabs down the left side of your page. You can choose which ones to display by clicking **More** and then **Manage Tabs,** where you will be able to drag and change the position of your app. It is obviously important to display the most important app in first position so it displays both under your cover photo and as the first tab on the left of your page.

**Using Custom Apps to achieve your marketing goals**

Custom apps let you create pages of your own to help you promote your products and services. These apps are created by third party developers and there are literally thousands of apps available for Facebook business pages. (These are not to be confused with the apps that you can add to your personal profile, like games, etc.)

Custom Apps offer more marketing opportunities for your business page, more functionality, and more to help increase the way you interact with your audience. However, before you start adding apps, the most important thing you need to do is think carefully about what your goals are and which apps are actually going to help you achieve those goals and objectives. There are many bells and whistles available for you to add to your page, but there is no point in adding an app which is only going to pull your audience away from your main goal and objective.

If you want to create your own iframe application, you can do this yourself by installing the Facebook Developer Application which can be found at https://developers.facebook.com/

Here are some more examples of custom apps that you can add to your page:
A custom welcome page with opt-in to catch fans (THIS IS ABSOLUTELY ESSENTIAL. More about this in the next section.)

- A store to sell your products
- Webinar sign up
- Your YouTube Channel
- Welcome page
- Sales coupons
- Sync & display your Twitter feed or Pinterest account

- Your webpage and your products
- Display location maps
- A staff page with images of your team
- An event announcement
- A competition or contest app
- Pull in your pins from Pinterest
- Pull in your posts from Google +
- Add a SlideShare app
- If you are a restaurant, you can add reservations through Opentable
  - Add an Etsy app and share your Etsy shop on Facebook
  - Create polls
  - Automatically stream your Flickr stream into Facebook
- Publish your blog post so they automatically display on your timeline

**Creating Facebook custom pages and tabs using iframes on Facebook**

Facebook allows you to create a custom tab on your page with an iframe application. This is where your index page is not actually hosted on Facebook but another server. An iframe application allows you to embed an external web page into your custom Facebook page tab and lets you build any content you want inside your tab using HTML, javascript, and CSS. You can also have forms, images, and videos. Basically anything that can be created on a website can be brought into Facebook.

The Thunderpenny static HTML iframe tabs application is a free third party application that makes it very easy to customize a Facebook page even if you have little or no technical know-how. Simply type "static HTML iframe" into the Facebook search box and it will come up with a grey star logo. You then need to follow the simple instructions to install the application. You can add images, forms, and videos. They offer online tutorials with instructions on how to do this at www.thunderpenny.com

There are also many other third party applications available which are really easy to install and use with simple drag and drop features. All the following providers offer apps like this: www.heyo.com, www.involver.com, www.shortstack.com, www.wildfireapp.com, and www.tabsite.com. They certainly take away the headache if you do not have the technical know-how to build HTML Pages. You can also find apps by searching in the Facebook search page. You need to check whether the apps use adobe flash, as apps with adobe flash cannot be displayed on an iPhone, iPod, and iPad.

**How to add apps to your page**
Simply visit any of the app websites, select the app you want to install, and follow the directions through a simple installation process. Once you have completed the installation process the app should appear on one of the tabs just under the cover photo. If you decide to delete the app, it is very straightforward. Simply click the cross to the right of the app and it will be removed.

If you want to create your own iframe application then you can do this yourself by installing the Facebook Developer Application. You can find it at https://developers.facebook.com/

**Displaying and viewing your apps**
You can display two custom apps under your cover photo and if you wish to add more apps, they will be displayed by clicking **More** under the cover photo and also on tabs down the left side of your page. You can choose which ones to display by clicking **More** and then **Manage Tabs,** where you will be able to drag and change the position of your apps.

**Changing the text on your custom tabs**
To change the text on your custom tab simply click **Settings** and **Apps** and then under the custom tab image, click **Edit Settings.**

## Adding images to custom tabs

Adding custom images to your tabs is a really effective way of attracting users to your custom pages. To do this, you need to create some eye catching images which fit in with your brand and add a clear call to action. You can upload a JPG, GIF or PNG file. The size of the image must be 111 x 74 pixels. To upload or change an image, click **Settings.** Go to the app listing, click on **Edit Settings,** and then **Change** where it says **Custom Tab Image.**

## Changing the position of the custom tabs

You need to think carefully about which tabs are most important and which ones you wish to appear under your cover photo. You can choose up to two which will display under your cover photo. Any others you add will be features under the **More** tab. You can manage the position of your tabs by clicking **More** and then **Manage Tabs,** and you can then drag your apps into position.

## Finding the URL to your custom page

If you wish to direct your users to a particular page, simply click **Settings, Apps,** and then **Link to this tab** under the App description.

## CREATING CUSTOM PAGES FOR YOUR OPT-IN OR A CONTEST

Adding an opt-in form to your Facebook page is absolutely essential if you want your campaign to succeed, and transferring your fans from your page to your opt-in should be your main marketing goal. With Facebook's new algorithm, which is making it more and more difficult to reach your fans organically, it is absolutely essential to get them onto your email opt-in at the very first opportunity. Once your fans have opted into your email list and given you permission to contact them on a regular basis, this is where you are going to win. Email is where you convert your fans into your customers.

Facebook users do not generally like to leave the platform so when a new fan arrives at your page, it is really important to capture their email address on Facebook rather than sending them to an exterior landing page and then losing them. To set up your email opt-in on Facebook you will need to build a custom page with a compelling offer to encourage your audience to sign, together with a sign-up form. You can easily create this with the 'Static HTML iFrame app' or use one of the many other third party apps like: www.pagemodo.com, www.heyo.com, www.wishpond.com, or www.leadpages.com . There are also many email providers who will provide an app for this which is easily integrated with your email capture form. These providers include: www.icontact.com, www.constantcontact.com, www.aweber.com, or www.mailchimp.com .

## Creating a competition or sweepstakes

A very effective way of capturing fans for your page and creating buzz is to create a competition or sweepstakes. Facebook has relaxed their rules considerably in regards to competitions so you can now run a competition on your page's timeline but not your personal timeline. You can either create your own competition or use a third party to do this for you. All this will be covered in detail later.

## SETTING UP A STORE ON FACEBOOK

There are three ways that you can set up a store on Facebook:

## A Storefront

You display your products with buy buttons on an app on your page which is connected to your website store. When the customer clicks the buy button they are then transferred to your website. Companies like http://storefrontsocial.com offer simple integration and sometimes a free trial.

## A Facebook Store

This is when all the activity takes place on Facebook and customers do not have to leave Facebook Page to purchase an item. There are many third parties that create online stores within Facebook. Simply type in 'Facebook Store application' into Google search or use a company like www.ecwid.com

## Selling directly from your newsfeed

You can sell products directly from your news feed by adding photos and directing customers to the URL of your external website or you can use a third party app to do this for you. You can also create an album with your Facebook products, enter the details and pricing and links to your website. www.rocxial.com is a third party app which enables you to sell products through Facebook news feed and photos.

## ADDING STARTER CONTENT AND MILESTONES

As mentioned earlier, Facebook allows you to add a start date which can be any date before you actually created your page. This allows you to create interest or a story behind your business before you actually start. This is also a good way of letting your visitors to your page know how long your business has been trading for.

Milestones are key moments you decide to highlight on your page. They have a flag icon and use up the full width of the News Feed with a lovely big image. Facebook creates your first milestone for you, and you can edit this by hovering over the top right hand corner of the milestone box and add a story and a photo, if desired.

A milestone could be anything from the opening of a business, the launch of a product, the launch of a website, or participation at a meaningful event or trade show. By adding milestones to your timeline you will add interest and depth to your page. To create a milestone simply click on **Offer/Event** on the top right of your page and then select 'Milestone'. Milestone images display at 843 pixels wide 403 pixels tall. You can use your own photos or use photos from stock photo sites or free photo sites such as Flickr.

# CHAPTER FIVE

## *HOW TO BUILD YOUR AUDIENCE ON FACEBOOK*

ONCE YOU HAVE created your page, added all your custom pages, a Facebook store if needed, and your opt-in page, you will be ready to publish your page and start building a highly targeted audience of fans for your page together with quality leads for your business.

Your main aim should be to use Facebook as a way to source traffic, create a relationship, and then drive them to take action either on or off your Facebook page on a Facebook store, on to your website, a landing page for an email sign up, sales page, video demonstration, or on your blog.

The more fans you have on your page the more potential you have to drive traffic to your website, especially when you crossed the 1000 fans milestone. Also with the introduction of Graph Search, fans are more important than ever. It is becoming evident that the more fans you have on your page the higher you will rank on a Facebook search.

Building an audience can seem like a very daunting process at first. However, building a sizeable audience in a short amount of time is possible and very rewarding when you see the number of fans (potential customers) growing on your page. But do not be misled into thinking it is going to be easy. As much as you may like to think that as soon as anyone sees your Facebook icon on your website they are going to like your page, it doesn't always work like that. Here are some strategies for you to use to build a highly targeted audience:

## Add your page to your personal profile

When you add your page name to the **Work and Education** section of your personal profile, it lets anyone viewing your profile see the name of your page. When they hover over the page name they will be able to see a mini image of your cover photo and they can 'like' or message you. Simply start to type your page name into the **Work and Education** section and your page name will display in the drop down for you to click on.

This is incredibly useful if you are networking and 'liking' other business pages on Facebook. When the owner of that page sees you have 'liked' their page, they may very well check out your profile, see you have a page, and may reciprocate by 'liking' your page too. Reciprocating by 'liking' your fans' pages is a very good practice. Supporting your fans this way goes a long way in building relationships, especially when you start engaging with their content.

## Invite your friends

Now your page and your personal profile are ready, and you can invite your Facebook friends. Simply go to your page, make sure you are using your page as yourself, and then click on **Build Audience** and then **Invite Friends**. You can select whoever you want to and send them an invitation to 'like' your page.

## Invite your email contacts

What better way to build relationships with your current contacts than inviting them to your Facebook page. Simply go to your page and, by using your page as yourself, click **Build Audience** and then **Import Contacts** and invite your contacts.

## Share your Page

This is another great feature within Facebook to build your audience. You can share your page on your own timeline by simply clicking **Share** on your cover photo. You can share it on your own timeline, on a friend's timeline, on another page you manage, or in a group.

## Create a free offer

Offering something free like an ebook or report can help increase the number of 'likes'. You used to be able to install something called a 'Like Gate' where people had to 'like' your page to get your offer, but unfortunately Facebook has stopped this now. However, all is not lost. You can still ask users to submit their email address to obtain your offer, and this can easily be set up with an app. Often email service providers will provide an easy-to-install application to catch email addresses, and you can add an image and text to promote your offer. Using other social networks like Twitter to direct people to your Facebook page can work very well. Simply ask followers to join you on Facebook by directing them to your free offer.

## Promote your page with a Facebook ad

Facebook advertising is a highly effective way of building your audience and lets you reach people who are not yet connected to your page. Because Facebook holds so much information about their users, they have made finding your target audience incredibly easy. You can target by age, gender, location, marital status, and interest. To advertise, simply click **Create Ad** from your personal profile and then select your page and the option **Page likes**. You simply design your ad by choosing your headline, text, image, and the page you want them to land on. You can then select the audience that you want to advertise to and your daily budget and you are ready to start promoting your page.

When people see your ad they can either 'like' it from the ad or click on the page link to see your page. If you have an offer on one of your pages then it would be a good idea to send them to that page and capture them with your opt-in.

When you are creating your ad you will see a tick next to the words **Sponsored Stories**. Sponsored stories help businesses promote word-of-mouth recommendations on their page by promoting the actions taken by their fans and making them more visible to their friends. For instance, if you have activated sponsored stories on your page and a Facebook user was to either check your page or 'like' your page, then their friends would see this action taken on the right side of their News Feed. This is an incredibly effective form of advertising because it creates social proof and word-of-mouth advertising, which is the most powerful.

## Post really good content

If you are posting really good content and your fans are engaging with that content by 'liking', commenting, and sharing, these actions will show up in their friends' News Feed which will help to encourage others to 'like' your page and join in the conversation. You need to make sure you are regularly creating the right type and balance of content that will appeal to your target audience.

## Use images in your posts

The introduction of larger images in the new News Feed design is really good news for businesses, and wherever possible you should use images to promote your posts. All the statistics show that images receive the most engagement and are far more likely to be shared than text only posts. You can either use your own photos or use stock photos or other photo sites like Flickr, as long as you first check the licenses for using these free images. For branding purposes it's always a good idea to add a small logo, Facebook page name, or watermark on your images.

## Create a competition or sweepstakes

To help attract people to their Facebook pages, more and more companies are giving away prizes in Facebook sweepstakes and contests. This type of promotion can be incredibly effective, and since Facebook has relaxed their rules concerning competitions, you can now run them on your timeline without having to use a third party application. To see Facebook terms about running contests please follow this link http:// www.facebook.com/page_guidelines.php#promotionsguidelines

There are a great number of companies that can help you with your competition such as: www.woobox.com, www.pagemodo.com, www.offerpop.com, www.strutta.com, www.wildfireapp.com, www.votigo.com, and the list goes on and on.

## Be Social

Being active on Facebook, commenting, and sharing other people's posts will increase visibility of your profile and your business page. Going to other pages and posting helpful comments is a sure way of getting people to come over and see what you are about. You can select whether you want to comment as yourself or your page by clicking the 'gear' icon at the top right of your page. This is particularly good for personal brands which have their own photo for their profile photo rather than a logo, as people much prefer to connect with a face.

## Use embedded posts to drive engagement

Facebook now lets you actually embed public posts in your blog and website by simply adding a line of code. To find the code simply go to the relevant post and open the drop down menu by clicking the arrow on the top right of your post and then click **Embed Post**. Embedding a post which has had lots of comments and 'likes' on it, will not only help create social proof but also help encourage others, who are not fans of your page, to 'like' your page. If you have a video, uploading it to Facebook and then embedding it on your website will increase the possibility of more people commenting on your video and increasing your reach too.

## Use Facebook groups to grow your audience

Finding your Facebook audience is made really easy with Facebook search and you can find all sorts of interest groups, pages, and people relating to your niche. By entering the relevant keywords into the search box at the top of your page Facebook will come up with a list of results relevant to your search and you can then filter the search information into various categories: groups, people, places, pages, events, etc. Joining groups in your niche and then joining in the community will not only help you make new connections, but you can post links to your blog posts or your Facebook page if the content is relevant.

## Leave comments on blogs, articles, and forums

If you are leaving relevant and interesting comments on other people's blogs, you can also leave an invitation to connect with you on your Facebook page. You may even get the blogger themselves.

## Promote your page on your blog

Writing a blog article about your Facebook page, and giving your readers reasons and an incentive to join, is a really effective way of promoting your page.

## Add your Facebook page to all your promotional and sales materials

Make sure you add your Facebook URL to any literature, business cards, brochures, shop signs, your transportation, or any other promotional material you produce. Make sure you have set up your Facebook username so it's easy for people to remember. You can also download Facebook table tents and stickers here http://fbrep.com//SMB/tent-cards-self-serve.pdf for promotion at your business place.

## Make Google Adwords work for you

Google Adwords can be a very effective way of finding new fans and then directing them to a specific page for a competition or a 'like' gate with a compelling offer. With Google Adwords you can find people who are actually looking for your specific product, and your page will not only offer them social proof that your business is bona fide but also give you the opportunity to stay in contact with them. This is a really good way to get Adwords to work for you. If you offer them an incentive to like your page, you can carry on the relationship with them on Facebook and have more chance of converting them into a customer than by just sending them to your website where they will more than likely disappear.

## Integrate Facebook with current advertising

Using Facebook in conjunction with magazines or newspaper advertising can really increase the effectiveness of your advertising. By adding your Facebook URL together with a good incentive for them to like your page you can continue a relationship that otherwise would have been lost.

## Encourage fans to ensure your updates show up in their news feeds

Because of Facebook's algorithms, your Facebook fans probably will not get to see all your posts unless they have switched on **Get notifications**. To do this you simply hover over the arrow where it says **liked** and click on **Get Notifications**. It's a good idea to encourage your fans to select this so they don't miss out on any of your updates. You could do this by announcing that you have something really exciting coming up in the near future and if they want to make sure they hear about it then they need to switch on **Get Notifications**.

## Add your Facebook handle to other social networks

Inviting your followers from Twitter or other networks to like your Facebook page is a really good way of increasing your 'likes'. Once in a while you can tweet about something that is happening on your Facebook page which will hopefully entice your followers to go over and have a look.

## Promote your offers and competitions on other networks

Posting content on your other networks is a great way to pull those users over to your Facebook page. For instance, if you are running a competition or offer on Facebook, make sure you pin your image on Pinterest and tweet about it on Twitter.

## Send a direct message to your Twitter followers

Some people are totally against sending direct messages on Twitter, but this can work in directing your Twitter followers to your opt-in page with a compelling offer. You can set up automated direct messages too.

## Join a LinkedIn Group

There are groups that exist on LinkedIn that are primarily set up to increase your 'likes' on Facebook. This may be good or not, depending on who your target audience is, but it can definitely help increase the number of your 'likers' and if you are selling B2B, this could be particularly good for you.

## Status tagging (shout-outs)

Tagging is when you mention someone in a status update or comment by using the @ sign before their name or page name. When you start writing the person's name, a pop up will appear and you can choose the correct person or page you wish to tag. This will create an instant link. The post to which you added their name or page name to may then be added to their timeline, and any user who clicks that link will be taken to their timeline. When you tag someone they will receive a notification, which is a great way of drawing attention to your page or profile. Also, if you or a friend tags someone in a post or photo which is set to **friends or more,** the post will be visible to their friends as well. You can use this to share other people's content and then tag them in the status update. If you or your page does get tagged, it is a really good practice to go back and thank the person who tagged you.

Another way of using this feature is that if you have photos of events, you can make a folder and then ask your fans to tag themselves in the photos. This is a great way of increasing your reach through their friends' News Feeds.

## Invite your fans to leave their Facebook Page URL

This is particularly good if you are selling B2B. People love to network and love any opportunity to promote their business. Inviting people to network on your page is an excellent way of increasing likes and a great way of showing how much you value your fans. You can do this on a specific day of the week or every month. By creating a special branded image to promote this you can also widen your reach when fans share your image.

## Use Facebook promoted posts

Promoting your posts with **promoted posts** is an excellent way to increase your reach. You can promote to people who already 'like' your page and to their friends or to a selected audience that you can choose. You will find more details about promoted posts later on.

## Add Facebook badges to your website or blog

Facebook has a great little feature called **Badges**. Badges make it easy for you to show off your Facebook profile, as well as your latest status updates, on your website or blog. Simply visit this page. http://www.facebook.com/badges/

## Connect your Facebook page with Twitter

To connect your Facebook page with Twitter simply visit here www.facebook.com/twitter . Once you have connected them, all your Facebook posts will go to Twitter with a link back to your Facebook page.

## Add your Facebook URL to your videos

Adding a link to your Facebook fan page from any videos you may have on YouTube or Vimeo is a great way of increasing you page 'likes'. If you have a YouTube channel and your main goal on Youtube is to increase your Facebook 'likes' then leave a comment with an incentive to go over and become a fan of your Facebook page.

## Add a QR code

You can generate a QR code for your Facebook page, and many sites offer this for free. Once you have your QR code you can place this on any printed material so it can be quickly scanned and your Facebook page 'liked'. This is also great if you are a local business. You can encourage people to 'like' your business page by simply scanning the QR code into their mobile. You can easily set up your QR code by using an app called 'Visual QR code generator'.

## Encourage people to check in at your business

With the introduction of the nearby tab and check-in, Facebook offers their users even more opportunities to find businesses near to them and also offers business owners more opportunities to be found. If a user checks-in at your business it will show up in their friends' News Feeds. By using Facebook offers you can create offers and give your fans an incentive to check-in at your business.

## HOW TO PROMOTE YOUR PAGE WITH SOCIAL PLUGINS

Social plug-ins increase the visibility of your page outside Facebook and increase the opportunity for people to 'like' your page. Plug-ins basically pull the Facebook experience into your website or blog and create social proof, by letting users see which of their friends have already 'liked', commented on, or shared on your Facebook page. For example, if you visit a website and see your friend's photo on the Facebook plug-in, or if they have commented on the page, you're probably more likely to take interest in that website, 'like' the page too, or buy the product.

Facebook offers eleven social plug-ins, which are detailed below. All the plugins can be found at this link http://developers.facebook.com/docs/plugins/ with instructions on how you or your developer can install them into your website or blog.

**The Like Button** lets users share pages from your site back to their Facebook profile with one click. The action will appear on their timeline and in their friends' News Feeds.

**The Send Button** allows users to easily send content to their friends. It allows users to send a personal message to a friend, group, or email. It's a good idea to put the "send" button next to the "like" button.

**The Follow Button** lets a user subscribe to your public updates on Facebook.

**Embedded Posts** allows you to embed any public post into your website or blog.

**The Share Button** allows people to share to Facebook and share with particular friends, groups, or in a private message.

**The Comments Plug-in** allows your users to comment on any piece of content on your site. The post will appear on your website as well as in the user's News Feed on Facebook. You can put this plug-in in as many places as you wish, including particular product pages on your website or blog site.

If you are commenting on a website or blog post you can post as yourself or as your page, which is a great opportunity to gain visibility for your page.

**The Activity Feed** plugin shows the most interesting recent activity on your site, using actions ('likes' and recommends) by your friends and other people.

**The Recommendations Feed** displays the most recommended content using actions by your friends or other users.

**Recommendations Bar** allows your website users to 'like' content, get recommendations, and share what they're reading with their friends. When a user 'likes' some content or an article on your blog or website, it shows up in their News Feed and their friends' News Feeds.

**The Like Box** allows you to see how many people 'liked' the page, how many of your friends 'liked' it, and you can view the recent posts. It allows you to 'like' the page without visiting it.

**The Login Button** shows the profile pictures of the user's friends who have already signed up for your site in addition to a login button. The login button is useful as it gives you information about the audience you are attracting to your blog or website.

**The Registration plug-in** allows users to easily sign up for your website with their Facebook account.

**The Facepile** plug-in displays the Facebook profile pictures of users who have 'liked' your page or logged in at your site. This is great for social proof.

There are also third party developers that create plug-ins which can be integrated into your page and ones that include plug-ins for multiple social platforms.

## HOW TO USE FACEBOOK GRAPH SEARCH TO BUILD YOUR AUDIENCE

Facebook has been slowly rolling in its powerful graph search, and it is currently available to people using Facebook desktop in English.

Graph search lets you carry out more detailed searches and find out more information on Facebook than ever before by letting you find connections between people, places, and things. For instance, you could search for friends with common interests or friends of friends in a certain city.

With graph search you can also look for particular posts and filter posts by author, keywords, location, and comments. Some filers have drop downs that let you refine your search even further. You can also continue to search for keywords and you will see suggested people, photos, pages, and apps that match your keywords. You can put keywords together for things that interest you, for example, restaurants that your friends like. In your search results you will see unique results based on your connections to people, places, and things.

Graph search has opened up even more targeting opportunities for marketeers offering searches with social relevance and has really let them drill down further with searches to find their ideal target audience. Here are some examples of the sort of searches you can perform with Facebook graph search. However, the combinations you can search on are endless.

**Find groups than your fans are in:** You can search for groups that people who have 'liked' your page have joined and that relate to your page in some way. This can help you network among people with similar interests. For example, "groups of people who like _ _ _ _ _ _" ( Page name)

**Find pages your fans 'like':** Identify other pages your fans 'like', for example, "Pages liked by people who like _ _ _ _ _" (page name).

**Find friends who have not 'liked' your page yet:** You can put a search query in for the friends who 'like' your page and then you'll be able to work out more easily which of your friends have not 'liked' your page and then send them an invitation.

**Find people who 'like' a particular page:** Graph search will show you who 'likes' a particular page, even if they are not your friends.

**Find pages 'liked' by particular people or pages:** This can help you interact even more with particular people or influencers. You can even sort by gender, age, and location.

**Find employees of certain companies:** For example, you could find out which pages the employees of a particular company 'like'.

**Find common interests:** You can find out more about your fans' interests and then determine which similar interests your fans have. This can help you produce the right content for your fans. Also, when it comes to advertising you can use this information to target people with particular interests.

# CHAPTER SIX

## CONTENT IS KING ON FACEBOOK

ONCE YOU HAVE prepared your page, started to gain 'likes,' and build your audience, this is only the beginning. Once users have 'liked your page, it is unlikely that they will return to your page. In fact, nearly 90% of fans will never return again. In order to build a thriving community of brand advocates and customers who want to share your content, sign up to your newsletter, and buy your products, you are going to need to build trust, loyalty, and likeability. The only way to do this is by communicating with them on a regular basis in the right way and by consistently delivering the highest possible quality content which will grab their attention, appeal to their interests, and add real value to their lives. Once your fans start engaging with your content, you will start building trust and start to convert them into customers.

Even when you start posting on Facebook it is unlikely that your posts are going to be seen by every one of your fans in their News Feed every time, unless you are paying for promoted posts. This is simply because Facebook uses an algorithm called Edgerank, which determines what does and does not show up in a user's timeline. They know that because of the sheer volume of content posted that if their users were to see every post it would ruin their viewing experience. Facebook devised the algorithm to create the best possible experience for their users, and Edgerank helps to ensure that users see what is most important to them and what has the greatest value. There are three variables that are measured to make up this algorithm and these are: affinity, weight, and time decay.

**Affinity:** Affinity measures the relationship between the viewer and the creator of the content. The closer the relationship, the higher the score. So the more one of your fans interacts with your content, the more likely your posts are going to show in their News Feed.

**Weight:** Weight measures the value carried by different types of content and the way users engage with that post will also affect the score.

**Time Decay:** Time Decay is about the age of the post. The older the post, the lower the score. This is what helps your News Feed to stay full of fresh, new content. Approximately 75% of engagement takes place within the first five hours and 60% within the first three hours. The value of the post will decrease as time goes on.

One of your main goals for creating content for Facebook is going to be producing the highest quality content for your audience so that they will engage with that content, thereby creating the highest possible Edgerank score. The higher your score, the more fans will see and engage with your posts. You can check your Edgerank score at this link www.edgerankchecker.com

In order to create the right content you are going to need to have a real understanding of your target audience and deep insight into what interests and motivates them. Once you have this information and put this together with the strategies in this book, there is no reason why you cannot build a thriving community of advocates for your brand on Facebook. In this chapter you are going to learn about the different types of posts, content, and tips on how to help you create the best experience for the fans so you can receive the highest engagement and highest Edgerank.

## 35 CONTENT IDEAS

With the competition out there on the Internet for attention, the only way you are going to win is with high quality content. Content really is king on Facebook. This is even more important now since Facebook is decreasing the number of posts from pages which are visible in the News Feed. You may be wondering how you are going to consistently produce and deliver compelling content to your audience on a regular basis for the foreseeable future. However, once you have picked your topic of interest, you will be surprised how one idea will lead to another and you will be able to find numerous pieces of content to create and post. Here are some ideas for content that can be adapted to any type of business or topic:

## 1. Relatable content

Relatable content is one of the best and most shared types of content. Relatable content is anything that your target audience can relate to and identify with. It's when your audience sees a piece of content and immediately thinks, "Yes, I can relate to that and this is exactly the way I feel when this happens." It's incredibly powerful because this content is immediately communicating to your audience that you understand them and you feel their pain or joy and can empathize with them. With relatable content you are communicating with them on quite a deep level, which all helps to build relationships and trust. This is why Someecards is so successful. Most of their content is relatable.

## 2. Emotive content

Evoking an emotional response is an essential ingredient to successful viral content marketing. If you create content that evokes a strong positive emotional response it will help your audience associate that emotion with your brand. Content like this is very memorable, and if you can make people feel something by posting an image, text, or video, this can really help in building your brand and creating powerful associations. Evoking any of the primary emotions, be it surprise, joy, fear, sadness, anger, or disgust, is a certain way to get people sharing your content.

## 3. Educational content

Posting informative content about your subject is invaluable. This will help you to stand out as a thought leader and expert in your field. If your content is valuable and useful, your followers are likely to keep coming back for more and are likely to share your content too. Remember, your audience is looking to find and share valuable content with their friends and customers, too, and will want to be associated with any compelling content you create.

## 4. Informative
This could be about letting your followers know about something that is happening, like a webinar, a trade show or event in the area, a special offer, or any information that will be of use or value to them.

## 5. Entertaining/amusing content
Social media is all about being social and having fun. People love sharing funny stuff. Even if you did not create it yourself but you think it is going to appeal to your target audience then share it. The aim here is to amuse and entertain your audience. Humor is a winner all around. Not only does humor break down barriers, it is also more likely to be 'liked' and shared.

## 6. Seasonal Content
Posting content related to important holidays and annual celebrations is a really good way to stay connected with your audience. If you have an international audience, being aware of their holidays and religious celebrations will go a long way in building relationships.

## 7. Inspiring and motivational content
The truth is everyone has a bad day sometimes and needs a little bit of motivation or cheering up. A motivational quote will help to lift your audience and can really help to connect with them. If you know what your audience wants, what they aspire to, and what their frustrations are, then it is likely that you will be able to motivate them by posting content which inspires them. These types of posts are also very shareable, especially if put together with a colorful and inspiring image like a

cartoon or photo.

## 8. Employee and behind-the-scenes content

If you have news about your employees and the great things they are doing, then post it. Maybe they have been involved in a fundraiser or won an employee of the month award. Giving your audience a behind-the-scenes view of your business helps to keep your business and brand looking real and authentic, and it adds human interest.

## 9. Customer Content

Having a member of the month or including news or content about a customer's business is a great way to spark interest in your posts. Sharing a customer's content not only shows you value your audience but that you can also encourage them to do the same. If you are B2B, you could also invite your audience to network and let them share their page on your page once a month or once a week. This is a great way to offer them value. It also creates loyalty, keeps your page in their mind, and keeps them coming back again and again to visit your page.

## 10. Shared Content

While it's great to post most of your own content, don't be afraid to share other people's content as long as it is relevant. The more valuable content you share, the more valuable you will become to your audience and the more likely they will be to keep coming back for more. Sharing content is also incredibly important in building relationships with your fans. They are going to be far more open to your brand if you are supporting theirs.

## 11. Statistics

People love statistics which relate to their niche. If your business is B2B then posting statistics can gain a great deal of interest, especially if they are displayed in a visually appealing way, perhaps with an infographic or graph. They are often shared if they are translated into a useful tip for your followers.

## 12. Questions

Asking questions about subjects your audience may be interested in is a great way to encourage comments, interaction, and community. People love to share their opinions and thoughts and love the opportunity to communicate, contribute, and be heard. Even if you are posting an image or video, it's a really good practice to ask a question.

## 13. Top Ten lists

People love lists about who or what is top or best. Lists spark interest and this probably because people like to compare their choices and judgements with others. Some may like to see that their opinions match others and feel they are right in that choice, and others may feel comforted by the fact their choices are not the same and they are unique.

## 14. Controversial

Posting a controversial statement can spark great conversation and interaction. Remember, people love to voice their opinions, have input, and be heard. It may be a good idea to stay out of the discussion here, as you do not want to lose followers and you need to be sensitive to your audience in order not to upset them, so be careful what topics you pick.

## 15. Special offers

Social media is a great way to get the message out about the special offers you have running, but you will need to be careful not to post them too often or they just appear like advertising and bad noise in your audience's News Feed. You need to make sure that what you are offering is of real value, that it is exclusive to your fans, and you are offering them a deadline to redeem the offer.

## 16. Contests and sweepstakes

Contests and sweepstakes are always a great way to gain popularity, grow your audience, build your brand, and build your opt-in email list. With contests, your audience can have great fun with your brand and they can also create high levels of engagement. There are so many different types of contests: photo and video competitions, sweepstakes, comment to win, polls, 'caption this' contests, photo contests, quizzes, and the list goes on. Creating and running contests will be covered in more details later on.

## 17. Voting polls & customer feedback

Creating a poll is a great way to encourage engagement on social media. Incorporating polls into your Facebook strategy can help give you a deeper understanding of your audience and also offer you valuable feedback about products or services. You can either ask your audience a question and ask them to 'like' or comment or use an app like 'Poll' or 'Polls for Facebook' or 'Polldaddy.'

## 18. Tips and tricks

Offering a weekly or daily 'Top Tip' can keep your audience hooked and returning again and again for the latest information and are a great way to increase loyalty and build relationships. Tips can be anything from instructions on how to do something to information about a useful app.

## 19. News and current events

Offering information about the latest news in your area or industry is a certain way to keep people interested and sharing your content. Being current and up-to-date with local news is really useful to your audience and it keeps your business looking fresh. To keep up-to-date with news, subscribe to News Feeds and blogs that offer news on your industry or your local area.

## 20. Negative content

People always like to hear about what not to do, for example: ten things not to do on a first date or ten things not to say in a job interview. The lists of possibilities for this type of post are endless and can create a great deal of amusement and interest.

## 21. Music, if you are a musician

If you are a band and want to promote your music, there is no better way to promote your material than by posting links to your music and videos on Facebook.

.

## 22. Q & A live session

You can host a live question and answer session on your page. This is a really good way to create conversation and engagement. It also creates a professional, informative, and caring image. You can do this by allotting and promoting a specific time for fans to post their questions in the comment section of your Facebook post. Or you could choose to ask them to post their questions and give them a day when you will be answering them. This way, you get more time to research. In both cases it's a good idea to post an image promoting the session.

## 23. Broadcast live

By using an application called Livestream, you can broadcast any live event to almost any social destination. You can also watch, 'like,' and share any event that may be of interest to your audience.

## 24. Fill in the blank posts

Getting your audience involved with your content is a very powerful way of creating engagement. Fill in the blank posts can be a way of creating engagement and conversation, for example:

I love going to _____ on my holidays because...

My Monday morning must have this_____

I always take _____ on vacation.

## 25. Caption this

Posting a photo and then asking your audience to caption it is a really effective and lighthearted way to drive engagement and you could also turn this into a contest. You can use images from stock photo sites or sites like Flickr Creative Commons. Make sure to choose images that will provoke interest and are humorous or inspiring.

## 26. Case studies

Case studies are a really effective way to demonstrate how something works with real examples. You can use case studies to show how your customers have used your products or services to benefit them in some way. You can also use them to demonstrate a principle or method of doing something by using other businesses as examples.

## 27. Internet Memes

Meme comes from the Greek word 'Mimema,' which means something imitated. An Internet meme is a style, action, or idea which spreads virally across the Internet. They can take the form of images, videos, or hashtags. There are plenty of tools and apps out there to help you create memes, such as www.memegen.com and imgur.com, which are popular ones.

## 28. 'Like' versus share votes

This involves combining two competing images in one post and then asking your audience to vote for which image they choose by 'liking' or sharing. This is a really quick way to expand your reach and get your brand out there. To be successful at this you really need to have a good subject and one that most people identify with.

## 29. Your blog

Creating regular blog posts is a very effective way of getting the fans onto your blog. Make sure you always include an image to provoke interest. Asking a question can create intrigue and curiosity.

## 30. Greetings

Simply posting an attractive image or wishing your fans good morning, good night, or to enjoy their weekend will go a long way in breaking the ice and building relationships. These types of posts help to make positive associations with your brand.

## 31. Testimonials and reviews

You may have received a review on Google Places or Foursquare or simply a message from someone. Posting about good things that people write or say about you contributes to your social proof and builds trust. Remember, people will believe more about what others say about your business than what you, as the owner, say about it.

## 32. Share something personal

People really like to connect with the person behind the brand. If you have your own personal brand, then this is really important. Sharing interesting positive snippets about your personal life can really help to build relationships and give an authentic feel to your brand. Sharing your plans for the day or posting the occasional photo of yourself can really help get your audience to know you.

## 33. Thank your fans

Thanking your fans for their engagement and support shows that you really value and appreciate them. This is not only courteous, but it will help make you stand out from the crowd and encourage your fans to participate and engage with your content in the future.

## 34. Ask your followers how you can help them

Keeping the lines of communication open by asking your fans what sort of content they want more of is another way of showing your fans that you are there to help them.

## 35. Your personal recommendations

Sharing anything of value with your fans, like a good book or a useful app, is a great way of offering value, and it helps keep your fans feeling positive about your brand.

## THE DIFFERENT TYPES OF MEDIA AVAILABLE

In order to create the best experience for your fans you are going to need to create a good balance of content using the different variety of posts available to you. Facebook gives you the opportunity to post text, images, videos, offers, events, and milestones.

## Images

"A picture paints a thousand words."

If you are already a Facebook user then you probably know that an image grabs your attention more than any other post in your News Feed. This is because most of us are visually wired and can identify with an image much more quickly than text. Statistics prove that pictures get more comments, shares, and 'likes' than any other post and that followers are far more likely to click on a link to a website, blog, or watch a video if the post contains a picture. According to Facebook, posts which contain a photo generate up to 180% more engagement. If you are posting a link to your blog or an article on your website, make sure you include a compelling image. You are far more likely to gain interest this way. Images not only get shared more, they also have huge viral potential, get remembered, and also create an emotional connection with your audience.

You don't have to be an expert photographer. You can find images from stock photos and also free sites like Flickr. (Be careful to check the license and what you are allowed to do with the images in terms of changing or adding text, etc.) Adding text can be achieved by using Photoshop or other online graphic design apps which are available and easy to use, like www.picmonkey.com . Some stock photo sites also offer you the functionality to add effects and text to your images.

The ideal size for uploading an image to your News Feed it 403 X 403 pixels. If you are linking to images outside Facebook, for example, on your website or blog, then you should aim to have images that are 1200 X 630, or greater, for optimal display on desktop and mobile devices. Larger images send more traffic to websites than smaller thumbnails.

## Videos

As with images, videos are highly shareable, have huge viral potential, and increase engagement. People love videos and a good video can offer a huge amount of entertainment, make learning more interesting, more fun, and easier to understand. Videos are also great at helping build relationships, trust, and rapport with your audience. There really is no better way of introducing yourself and building a personal connection with your audience than with video.

The type of videos you should be posting on Facebook are educational, informative, and entertaining and while there is room for the occasional product video, these really belong on your website or blog.

Facebook allows you to upload your video file and stream it directly on your timeline. You can post links to your YouTube videos or share other people's videos. If you want to upload a video to Facebook from your smartphone, you can do so by attaching it in an email and sending it to your unique Facebook email address. To add a caption, simply write it in the subject line of the email.

## Text

Whether you are posting a text only post, an image, or video, it is likely that you will be including some text to either introduce or describe your post. As a general rule of thumb, the shorter you keep it, the more engagement you will receive. While that is not to say that longer posts are unsuccessful, generally speaking, it is best to keep the majority of your posts shorter. According to Facebook, posts between 60–250 characters receive 60% more likes, comments, and shares.

While images are definitely more effective and receive higher engagement, there is still room for text only posts to deliver the occasional tip, a greeting, or to ask a question. There are some pages that are very successful at creating engagement with a large number of text posts, but in the end it always comes down to the quality of the content.

## Highlighted Posts

If you have a particularly important post or a really compelling image or infographic that needs space, using a highlighted post is a great way to draw attention. The highlighted post spans the whole width of the News Feed and is an excellent opportunity for you to showcase your story. You can really create the "wow factor" with a highlighted post.

To highlight your post, simply upload your image and hover your mouse on the top right of the post over the down arrow and a drop down menu will appear. Simply click the star on the top right of the post and the picture will span both columns of the News Feed. The perfect image size for a highlighted post is 843 X 403 pixels.

## Milestones

Milestones on Facebook are used to mark key moments or major events that you want to promote and showcase with your audience. When you create a milestone, it is displayed with a flag icon and automatically expanded to the width of your News Feed. You can use milestones to mark the opening of a business, the launch of a new product, or the launch of an event. The ideal size for a milestone image is 843 X 403 pixels and Facebook will automatically upload it as a highlighted post to span the width of the News Feed. However, you can choose to display it as a normal size post by clicking the highlight button. You can add a location, date, and story for a milestone post. A good tip for milestone posts is to tag as many people who were involved in the milestone as possible.

## Blog Posts

According to research, 70% of consumers click through to a website from a retail blog. Blogs are nearly essential now for any business who wants to get found on the Internet, and social media is another very effective tool to drive traffic to your blog. If you do not have a blog then you need to seriously consider creating one. There are numerous free and paid blogging platforms available and there is a whole chapter covering this very subject later on in this book.

## Infographics and diagrams

Infographics provide a fascinating way to present statistical information. They are engaging, very shareable, have huge viral potential, and make figures look far more interesting and easier to understand than a list of numbers. People love statistical information relating to their interest because it helps to confirm or affirm what they already may believe, and it helps to give them more confidence in what they are doing or selling. You do not have to be an expert graphic designer to create infographics. There are numerous applications available on the web which can help you do this. Facebook offers you the ability to post large and wide images with highlighted posts, which are excellent for infographics.

## Podcasts

Podcasting is a type of digital media usually comprising a series of audio, radio, or video files. You can subscribe to podcasts as you can to blogs and newsletters. For example, if you download a podcast on iTunes, every time the author produces a new one, iTunes will automatically download it. As with video, they are effective at helping to build trust with the listener and can also help you stand out as an authority or influencer in your niche. They encourage customer loyalty if they are produced on a weekly or very regular basis and are incredibly handy for people who are on the go and want to listen while traveling to work or on the way to a meeting. Facebook is the ideal place to promote your podcast.

## Cartoons

Cartoons work very well with humor and relatable content. Posting cartoons that your audience can relate to will help demonstrate that you understand and identify with them. They are a great ice breaker and highly shareable as well. Once shared, they are very likely to appeal to more of your target audience and are a great way to widen your reach. If you have an idea for a cartoon, there are sites like Fiverr.com where you can find creatives who offer this type of service at very reasonable prices.

### SlideShare

SlideShare is primarily a slide sharing site, but you can upload PowerPoint, keynote, pdf, and open office presentations. SlideShare is a great way to communicate your message, and it is very straightforward and easy to use. It is also another way to get your content rated, commented on, and shared. Your presentations can be embedded into Facebook and your website or blog.

### Ebooks & PDF documents

Turning your content into an ebook is a great way to present your content, and offering a free ebook is a really good way to build your opt-in lists and give your reader something of great value.

### Webinars

A webinar is like an interactive online conference or workshop. Webinars are a great way of interacting with your audience and building relationships. They can be used for presenting and training, selling a program or course, or answering questions from your audience. They can be saved and listened to at a later date for anyone who could not make the original date and time. Using Facebook to announce your webinar is a very effective way to promote your online event and get people to sign up.

## TOP TIPS FOR POSTING CONTENT ON FACEBOOK

Here are some invaluable tips for posting content on Facebook:

### Is this relevant to my audience?

Every time you post anything ask yourself this question, and if the answer is no, then don't post it.

### Post frequently

To create the greatest opportunity for your fans to see your posts you will need to post between 2-4 times a day. The average lifespan of a post is about three hours and the majority of engagement happens in the first hour. Some people may only view their Facebook page once a day. Therefore, balancing your content at different times of the day is going to boost your chances of having your post seen by more people. Having said this, quality will always win over quantity, so if you do not have anything really good then don't post it.

## Create compelling headlines and introductions

Make sure you always communicate why you are sharing and why you think your post will be particularly interesting to your audience. Not only will this grab your audience's attention, but it also helps to personalize your posts and start a conversation.

## Include a call-to-action

Facebook posts that include a call-to-action receive far more engagement than posts that do not. Your fans need a little nudge to remind them to 'like', comment, or share, and offering them a choice is very effective. For example, 'like' to agree or comment if you don't. You need to ask your fans to do what you want them to do.

## Questions

People are on social media to be social and interact, and people will interact with people other than their friends if they are given the opportunity to do so. One of the best ways to encourage this interaction is through asking questions. According to statistics, asking questions can double your engagement. These could be questions relating to business or non-business topics/subjects. Questions are great ice breakers, spark conversation, and increase engagement. Whether posting an image, video, or text, asking a question provokes discussion.

## Facebook hashtags

A hashtag makes a word, group of words, or phrase into a clickable and searchable link in the Facebook News Feed. Every hashtag has its own unique URL on Facebook, and when you click on one, you will see a feed of posts that include that particular hashtag. To create a hashtag simply put the hashtag sign before the word, or group of words, without leaving any spaces between the words. To make your hashtag easier to read you can capitalize the first letter of each word. Even though hashtags do not work on cellphones you can still post them and they will work on desktops. You need to be careful not to post too many hashtags in one post as it just begins to look uninteresting and your fans will lose interest in what is really being said.

The proper use of hashtags on Facebook will greatly benefit your campaign by increasing your reach on Facebook and giving you further opportunities for your content and page to be found. If you find popular hashtags relating to your topic or subject, using these will increase the possibility of your posts being found.

## Pin to Top

There may be some posts that you deem particularly important and want new users to see when they arrive at your page. When you 'Pin to Top' your post will appear at the top of your News Feed on the left and stay there for 7 days. At the end of the period you can pin it to the top again if you wish. To pin a post to the top of the page simply hover over the top right of the post, click on the pencil icon, and then click **Pin to Top**.

'Pin to Top' is a very handy little feature and you could also use it to tempt users to become fans by posting an image with a call-to-action. For example, 'Become a fan to receive the latest updates on…..xyz'. You could also use this function to drive new people to an offer, opt-in sign-up form, or an online or offline event like an exhibition or trade show. You could also use it to post a welcome video or a recording of your most recent webinar. Whatever your top promotional goal for the week is, make sure you use the 'Pin to Top' function to promote that goal.

## Promoted Posts

Using promoted posts is the only way to guarantee that your posts will appear in the News Feed of all your fans. By clicking **Boost Post** on the bottom right of your post you can choose to either promote your post to the people who already 'like' your page and their friends or to people you choose through targeting. The cost of your promoted post will depend on the number of people who see your post. You can watch the progress of your promoted post campaign as it runs, and you can stop your promotion at any time. Simply click on the heading **Promoted for $** at the bottom of the post and then click on the 'gear' icon on the bottom right in the next window which is displayed and then click **Stop Promotion**.

How frequently you use promoted posts will depend on your budget. In order to make the best use of your budget you will need to try and make sure you promote only those posts that are likely to create the most engagement. The best way to do this is to watch and see how your fans are engaging with a post before promoting it, and if it looks to be successful, promote it. Entertaining posts are usually the ones that receive the most engagement rather than the more sales-driven posts. However, if you have a really good offer, or have a particular action that you want your audience to take, then using this feature is a really good way of guaranteeing that as many people see it as possible.

When you promote a post, Facebook will automatically create a sponsored story. Friends of people who have taken any action on your post by either 'liking', commenting, or sharing will see that on the right side of their News Feed.

## Embedded Posts

Embedding your most popular post in your website or blog can really help to increase your reach and engagement and therefore help to increase your Edgerank score. Simply copy the URL of your post, visit this page, https://developers.facebook.com/docs/plug-ins/embedded-

<u>posts</u>, and then paste it into where it says **URL of post,** click on **Get code,** and paste it into your website or blog.

## Scheduling Posts

Facebook offers you the functionality to schedule posts in the future, and you can schedule posts for photos, texts, images, and videos. This can assist you in timing your posts and freeing you up so you can really keep on top of your Facebook posts. One day you may want to create images for inspirational quotes and you could then post all of these in advance for as far in the future as you wish. To schedule a post, simply complete your post and then click the clock symbol at the bottom left of the post and enter the year, day, and time. You can also schedule your posts using third party sites like Tweetdec, Hootsuite, and Buffer.

## Add emoticons

According to statistics, adding emoticons can increase engagement by up to 33%. It's probably not a good idea to add them to every post, but including these funny little images in the occasional post can really add a personal touch, which can result in more comments and shares.

## Add images to an album

Adding images to an album rather than directly to your News Feed can really help to increase engagement. When people see a large number of 'likes' on a post they are more likely to click the 'like' button. Because Facebook groups all the 'likes' for all the images into one total sum in albums, this is great for social proof.

# CHAPTER SEVEN

## CREATING EVENTS AND CONTESTS ON FACEBOOK

FACEBOOK EVENTS ARE a great way to share your events and even virtual events like the launch of a new blog, website or webinar.

## CREATING AND PROMOTING FACEBOOK EVENTS

Creating an event from your business page is like creating an event from your personal account, except you do not have the ability to send direct invitations to your fans and you cannot send Facebook emails to people who are attending. A way around this is to post your event on your own timeline, join your event from your timeline, and then invite your friends. When you post your event, the fans of your page will be able to invite their friends too.

To create an event on your page click on **Offer, Event +** on your timeline. Add the name and details of the event, the location, the date and time, and also a video or image. Images need to be at least 714 X 264 pixels. You also need to add the link where tickets can be obtained from, and this is where you can put the link to your external website. For business events, it is definitely advisable to have an event page outside Facebook, either on your website or a specific event website.

Facebook does not actually support ticket sales. The most popular ticket sales integration seems to be Eventbrite and Eventpal. Eventbrite offers you the opportunity to connect your events to Facebook and will include a link to your ticketing page, which will also be included as a link in your News Feed.

When you have created your event you can share it with your fans by clicking the **share** button on the top right of your page. Make sure you pin your event to the top of your page.

**Promoting your event**

To ensure maximum exposure of your event, there are strategies you can put in place to further promote your event, which are as follows:

- **Create buzz prior to creating your event:** Before you do actually create your event on your Facebook page it may be a good idea to create some buzz by announcing the event and advising your fans that more details will be posted soon.
- **Use you cover photo:** Your cover photo is a very powerful way to promote your event and draw the attention of new visitors to your page. You can either encourage your new visitors to click the cover image to be taken to an external link or create an arrow pointing to the events tab underneath the cover photo. When you add your new cover photo it will also show up in your News Feed for your fans to see.
- **Promote your event with Facebook Advertising:** When you create your event you will automatically be offered the opportunity to promote it. Simply click **Promote** and you will be sent to the **Event Responses** page where you can choose the audience you wish to target and your budget.
- **Promoted Posts:** A promoted post is a really effective way of promoting your event to all your fans and their friends, and you can target people who are not connected to your page as well. Simply use your event photo and click on **Boost post** and then make sure you pin this to the top of your page. Make sure you add a call-to-action and ask your fans to share the event.
- **Repost your event:** Reposting during the few weeks before your event at different times of the day will help make sure as many of

your fans get to know about your event as possible. You could also post different images and information about the event to keep your fans interested.

- **Create a Facebook offer:** You can offer a discount or some kind of benefit to your fans by posting an offer.
- **Invite your friends:** You can't invite your friends from your page, but if you join your event from your personal timeline, you can then invite your friends. Once your friends have RSVP'd, they will then be able to invite their friends, too, by using the **Invite Friends** tab on the top right hand side of the event page. Make sure, when posting about your event, you allow friends to invite their friends and make it clear to them they can do this.
- **Promote on all your marketing and other social platforms:** Make sure you put details about your event on all your blogs and websites and promote it on your other social media sites too.
- **Email your contacts:** You may have customers who are not fans of your Facebook page so be sure to let them know about your event too. Emailing your contacts also makes sure that as many people as possible see your announcement in case they did not see your post on Facebook.

## THE BENEFITS OF RUNNING A CONTEST

Many businesses have found running competitions on Facebook to be hugely successful. Facebook contests and competitions are a great way of both generating engagement and new leads for your business. Since Facebook relaxed their rules and are now letting businesses run competitions directly on their page, running a competition is a whole lot easier, less expensive, and much more available for smaller businesses. Previously you were only allowed to run a competition through a third party app. It's a good idea to check Facebook terms and conditions regarding promotions. For example, Facebook still does not permit 'liking' your page or sharing a post as conditions for entering. You also need to check the rules governing contests in your country or state.

Before creating your contest you need to be clear about what your goals are and what you want to achieve through running one. The main benefits for running a competition on your page are as follows:

- **You can build your audience:** A competition is the quickest and easiest way of increasing the number of 'likes' for your page. However, Facebook terms stipulate that you are not allowed to make it a condition to enter your contest. Simple sweepstakes competitions are very popular for increasing the number of 'likes' to your page.

- **Engagement:** Getting people to share your competition is a sure way to increase engagement and a way to improve your Edgerank. Running photo competitions can create huge engagement and a real buzz for a business with fans sharing and commenting on photos. Some third party apps offer the functionality to prompt entrants to share your contest every time they enter.

- **You can capture email addresses for your opt-in:** This is a huge advantage to creating a contest, and once your fans have joined your opt-in, this is a big step in converting them to customers.

- **Brand awareness and social proof:** Having a large number of 'likers' helps to build your social proof, and any promotion like this will help to increase awareness of your brand.

- **Reward your audience:** When you give your audience the opportunity to win something they really value, this helps to keep them interested, particularly if you offer everyone a money-off coupon as a reward for entering.

- **Drive traffic to your website:** You can create a competition with the aim of driving traffic to your website by asking your audience to find certain information about the products on your website and then complete an entry form.

## HOW TO CREATE YOUR COMPETITION OR CONTEST

There are two ways you can create your contest: either directly on your page or by using a third party app.

## Creating a competition directly on your page

Running your competition directly on your timeline is not only straightforward it is also less expensive. Contests can create a great deal of interest on your page, especially if you are asking for some sort of engagement or action to be taken on your page. Here are some ideas for creating contests on your timeline:

- **A comments contest:** You can post a photo and then ask your fans to comment on it. This is a really effective way of launching and creating buzz around a new product you may be about to launch.

- **Create a 'likes' contest:** The advantage of this type of contest is that it is very simple for people to enter. Simply ask your fans to 'like' a post for the chance to enter.

- **Caption this contest:** These types of contests are great fun and give your fans a chance to be creative. Simply upload a compelling image and ask your fans to write a caption. The most original captions wins.

- **Fill in the blank contest:** Another fun idea for your fans is to simply pick a subject relating to your brand and then write a sentence and leave a space blank for your fans to complete it.

- **Photo contest:** Photo contests are really popular. You can either ask fans to submit their photos by attaching them to a private message or ask them to post them on your wall.

- **Questions and answers contest:** This is a really good way of getting your audience to find out about one of your products. Simply ask your audience to answer a question relating to one of your products or services.

- **Ideas contest:** Get your fans to participate by asking them for their ideas to solve a problem. You may need ideas for the name of a new product. This type of competition not only increases engagement, it also shows you value your fans' opinions and can really make them feel part of your brand.

For best results, here are a few tips for running a contest directly on your timeline:

- **Post a good image:** Using a good image with a description will help tempt your fans to enter and share your contest. However, you are not allowed to make this a condition of entering.

- **Customize the tab for your contest page**

- **Create a competition image for your cover photo:** Make sure you direct people to where they can enter to win with an arrow to the custom tab.

- **Create a clear headline and call-to-action:** Make it clear in the first sentence of your post what you want your fans to do.

- **Add a clear description:** Make it really easy for your fans to understand how to enter and include a description of the prize. Remember to also include hashtags so your get found, for example: #contest, # competition #win #photocontest #sweepstakes.

- **Create a page to collect entries:** If your goal is to collect email addresses then you will need to create either a page on your website or a separate landing page.

- **Pick the ideal prize:** The type of prize you are going to offer is really important, and you should choose a prize which is related to your line of business. This way your contest is far more likely to appeal to your target audience and you will then attract fans who are going to be more likely to be interested in the type of product you offer. You could even create some buzz and engagement prior to launching the competition by asking your fans what sort of prize they would like to win.

- **Decide on the duration of the competition:** You will need to decide on the duration of the competition. With photo and video competitions, you will need to offer a longer time for entrants to carry out the task. With sweepstakes, the duration of the competition can be much shorter.

- **Keep competition rules clear and simple:** You can either include rules in the post or create an external website page for the rules of your competition and make sure you include the following:

The number of times a participant is allowed to join

The amount of time the winner has to claim their prize

The closing date

Who is eligible

How the winners will be selected

- **Include the term 'Void where prohibited':** This ensures you are in compliance with any country or state regulations banning your promotion.
- **Include details of how the winner will be chosen.**
- **Announce winners on your timeline:** For competition results you can now announce the winner on your timeline and require that entrants come back to the page to find out who the winner is.

## Creating your competition with a third party app

If you want to launch a competition without the worry of administering it yourself then using a third party is ideal. Apps have many advantages, especially if you want to attract a large number of entrants and want to collect emails and add sharing functionality. For larger audiences and sweepstakes, using a third party not only looks professional, it is easier to administer and you can also collect emails and add functionality for sharing your contest. Here are some of the features and benefits of using third party apps:

- **Look professional and sophisticated:** Third party apps can help to make your whole contest look both professional and **organized,** which helps to create trust with your entrants.
- **Email capture:** By using a third party app you can collect email addresses when your users enter the competition.
- **Include sharing functionality:** Third party apps often include a feature where your entrants are offered the opportunity to share the contest.

- **They select the winner:** Using a third party takes away all the administration involved in selecting and notifying the winner.
- **'Thank you' coupons:** You can easily create a thank you coupon for all your entrants so everyone is rewarded for entering. This also helps to drive sales conversions.

In conclusion, third party apps help you to get more 'likes', more engagement, more conversions, more shares, and more emails.

You can visit some of the following to check out prices and information: www.wishpond.com, www.binkd.com, http://www.easypromosapp.com, http://www.wildfireapp.com, www.votido.com, www.offerpop.com. Wildfire offers a great video demo which is really educational, and many of these providers offer case studies so you can see lots of examples of competitions.

## PROMOTING YOUR COMPETITION OR CONTEST

Whether you are creating your own contest directly on your timeline or using a third party app you will still need to gain the maximum exposure possible, here are some ways you can promote your contest:

- **Create Buzz prior to competition announcement:** To create some excitement and buzz before the competition is announced you could offer a teaser asking your fans to watch out for the new competition. You could also post a question and ask your fans what prize they would most value.
- **Create a promoted post:** Upload your image with text about your contest with a link to your competition landing page. You can promote your post to the people who 'like' your page and their friends and to a wider, targeted audience.
- **Create an ad on Facebook:** Creating a Facebook ad can widen your audience enormously. Simply click on the **Adverts Manager** from your page and then **Create Ad** on the top right.
- **Repost your competition:** Reposting at different times during the few weeks before your competition date expires will help to let as many people as possible see the competition in their News

Feed.

- **Announce your contest on all your other social platforms:** You can use hashtags on Facebook and Twitter so people who are looking for competitions will find you. You can use keywords like sweepstakes, competitions, contest, win, photocontest, etc.
- **Pin to top:** Make sure you pin your competition image to the top of your page so new visitors to your page will see it.
- **Change your cover photo:** Adding your competition image to your cover photo will ensure that any new visitors see your competition, and it will also appear in the News Feed of your fans.
- **Encourage your fans to share your event:** Adding a call-to-action in your post is a great way to prompt people to spread the word.
- **Promote on your website or blog:** Make sure you put a banner about your competition on your blog and website.
- **Email your contacts:** You may have customers who are not fans of your Facebook page, so be sure to let them know about your competition too. Emailing your contacts also ensures that as many of your fans as possible see your announcement, in case they did not see it in their News Feed.
- **Advertise with Google Adwords:** You can use adwords to drive traffic to either Facebook or a separate competition landing page.
- **List your contest on contest sites:** There are lots of websites where you can enter your contest details.
- **Promote offline:** Make sure you include details about your competition on any of your marketing material, at your point of sale, and on receipts or bills.

## Analyzing your results

Most third party applications let you analyze the results by giving information, and they can compare the effectiveness of your competition with Twitter. You will be able to see how the contest has affected your interaction on Facebook by viewing the insights and compare figures before and after the competition. Make sure you measure the number of new fans, contestants, 'likes' and shares per contest, sales of product, and visits to your website.

Tracking these figures will help you in creating new contests and bettering your results in the future. Measuring results will give you a good idea whether or not the contest worked. You may decide that you need to promote more on the weekend or at a certain time of the day.

# CHAPTER EIGHT

## DAY TO DAY ACTIVITY

THERE ARE CERTAIN things that you will need to do on a day-to-day basis to run your campaign on Facebook. It is a good idea to allot a specific amount of time and a particular time of day to do this. Here are some of the things you will need to do:

### 'Liking' your customer's pages

This is important if your customers are business owners themselves. 'Liking' their pages or following your customers will go a long way in building relationships. By 'liking' their pages, you are showing them that you are interested in what they have to say and also helping them to achieve their goals by helping to build their audience.

### Showing your audience you value and respect them

If you value and respect your audience they will probably love, respect, and value your business. Be kind, generous, offer as much help and value as possible, reply to their comments, and make it obvious that you value them and are listening to them. Don't be afraid to be yourself rather than a stiff brand with no personality.

Everyone is aiming for shares, 'likes,' and comments, so if you are helping others out by commenting and 'liking' their content, it is going to draw attention to your brand. Once they see you have taken an interest they are more likely to take an interest in your content. This is one area where the reciprocation rule works very well on Facebook. Engaging with content will also draw attention to you and your brand, and you will find that people will click on your name to find out who you are and they may very well subscribe to your channel. Be friendly to your audience, be chatty, authentic, genuine, and embrace the conversation. All this will all go a long well in building a positive image for your brand and will set you apart from others who are continually ambushing their audience with self-promotion.

## Follow influencers in your niche or 'like' their pages

Building relationships with key influencers in your niche is invaluable. Not only can you learn from their content but also these people can have literally 1000's of fans so when you start to interact with their content, you are exposed to their fans.

## Dealing with negative comments

Every business at some time will have to deal with negativity from followers. Hopefully if you have a good product then this is not going to happen too often. There are 'trolls' out there who have nothing better to do than post negative comments. The best thing to do with them is just ignore them, delete their comments, and block them. However, there will be real customers who have real concerns and complaints and may post negative comments publicly. There may also be people who really want to lash out to gain your attention as quickly as possible and spread the news to their friends too! You need to deal with complaints quickly and be as transparent and authentic as possible. The best thing to do is to apologize and say how sorry you are to hear of the inconvenience they have been caused and offer to continue the conversation and deal with their concern by either private message or telephone. You can then deal with this privately, give your customer the full attention they deserve, and decide on your next course of action or compensation.

# CHAPTER NINE

## ADVERTISING ON FACEBOOK

FACEBOOK HAVE CREATED a highly effective and user friendly advertising platform for their users which has been designed to help businesses advertise to their target audience. As reaching your audience organically (free) on Facebook is becoming more and more difficult paying for the attention on Facebook is becoming more and more necessary especially of you have a particular offer or promotion.

Because Facebook holds such a massive amount of information about their users, including: age, gender, location and interests, you can easily leverage the power of Facebook to reach your target audience. You can even target users based on the groups that users have joined and the pages they have liked, yes you can target the fans of your competition! And targeting adverts to fans of your own Page can really help to drive down the cost of your advertising considerably. You can use Facebook advertising to either advertise your Facebook page or to drive traffic to an external website or blog.

Depending on your advertising objective you can choose any of the following Facebook advertising options:

### 1.) Page post engagement ( Promoted Page Posts.)

Promoted posts ensure that your posts show up in the timeline of the people who have liked your page and their friends and also to a wider targeted audience if you wish.

**Page post photo**

Text 90 characters

Image Size 1200 x 1200 px

## Page post link ad
Text 90 characters
Link title 25 characters
Image size 1200 x 627 px

## 2.) Page Likes ( Get more likes)
You can create adverts to grow your audience on Facebook. This is incredibly important for succeeding on Facebook. Once you have people 'like' your page you have more opportunity to build trust and then convert then into customers.
Text 90 characters
Image size 1200 x 450 px

## 3.) Clicks to Website ( Get more clicks to your website)
Enable you to advertise an external website or blog.
Text 90 characters
Advert image size 1200 x 864 px

## 4.) Website Conversions
You can create adverts for particular actions for people to take on your website. You will need to use a conversion tracking pixel to measure your results.
Text 90 characters
Advert image size 1200 x 864 px

## 5.) App Installations ( Get more app users)
Offers you the opportunity to create an advert which encourages users to install your app.
Text 90 characters
Advert image size 1200 x 864 px

## 6.) App Engagement ( Increase app engagement)

Offers you the opportunity to create an advert to get more activity on your app.

## 7.) Event Responses ( Increase event attendance)

Offers you the opportunity to create adverts to promote an event.

Text 90 characters

Event Title 25 characters

Image Size 1200 x 450 px

## 8.) Offer Claims ( Create offers that can be redeemed in store)

Offers you the opportunity to either create an offer, or advertising an offer you have already created on your timeline.

Text 90 characters

Offer Title 25 characters

Image Size 1200 x 627 pixels

## Creating Your Facebook Advert

Creating your advert is really straight forward, Facebook takes you through a very simple step by step process. You will need to select or upload an image, create a headline and description, select your audience, decide if you want your advert to appear in News feed or alongside it and set your campaign budget. Here are some tips for creating your adverts:

- **Study other adverts** Have a good look at what adverts are appearing on your News feed and which ones attract your attention.

- **Image** Your image is the most important part of your advert, this is what will grab your audience's attention. If you are looking to increase your page likes then Facebook will automatically populate your advert with your Page's cover photo. If then you are going for an advert which is going to appear to the right of your News feed then picking a close up image is going to show up much better. You can also use clear readable type, or funny pictures. You can find images on Facebook in their library, or other stock photography sites, or search creative commons licensed images. You can use an online image editor like http://www.picmonkey.com to enhance, edit and add effects to your images, if your photoshop skills are not up to much.

- **Headline** You will need to use an attention grabbing headline and the maximum number of characters you can use is 25.

- **Text** ( 90 Characters) To create an effective advert you will need describe the most important benefit to your audience, create desire by offering a discount or free trial and then end with a call to action for example, 'click here to get this free offer' or 'click here to get this free ebook' or 'RSVP Now'.

- **Create more than one advert** It's definitely advisable to create more than one advert. This way once your campaign is running you can see which one is the most successful and use those that are performing better.

**Advert Placement**

Make sure your have chosen where you want to display your advert and you have three options:

- **Desktop News Feed**
- **Mobile News Feed ( Adverts placed on Mobile tend to do better)**
- **Right Column**

To get the most engagement then it is advisable to place on Desktop News feed and in Mobile News Feed.

**Selecting your audience**

You can define the relevant audience for your adverts by selecting from the following:

- **Location**
- **Gender**
- **Age**
- **More demographics** Demographic options include: Relationship Status, Education Level, Subject, School/University, Undergrad years and Workplaces.

- **Interests** When it comes to interests Facebook will provide a drop down menu of different interests and it is here where you can target people who have liked other pages too. Simply start typing in the name of the Page or Group and Facebook will offer you matches.

- **Connections** You can select people who are already connected to your Page or Group, app or event and their friends or you can exclude people who are connected to a certain Page, Group, app or event.

As you select Facebook will display the number of people you will be targeting. Your audience size should be proportional to your budget otherwise you will not reach everyone in your targeted audience. If you find you are targeting too few people with the interests you have selected then try and include related interests to widen your reach.

## Setting up your campaign and budget

Once you have created your adverts and selected your target audience you can set your campaign budget, this can be per day or over the lifetime of your campaign. You can either schedule your advert to run continually or set a start and end date. Next you need to bid and you can either bid for Page likes clicks or impressions. When you bid for impressions you pay for when people see your advert. Once you have completed this section you are ready to start advertising.

## CREATE, CAPTURE, CONVERT WITH FACEBOOK ADVERTISING

Throughout this book you will read numerous times about the importance of capturing the email addresses of your prospects and how important it is to obtain their email address by offering them a compelling offer on either a special Facebook landing page, your website or a separate landing page with a compelling offer. With the functionality available on Facebook and easy access to your target audience you can easily set up a lead capture system that works on autopilot and here is how you do it:

## Create your special free offer

Firstly you need to think of something that your target audience really want and it needs to be something they would consider really valuable, this could be a free ebook, a short video course or a Webinar about a really hot topic or a special money offer coupon. Webinars and videos can be incredibly effective as they help to create an immediate personal connection with your audience from the start. This can be extremely powerful as most of us like to buy from people they like and trust. When choosing your offer you need to ask yourself this one question: is this valuable enough that my ideal customer would pay for it? If your answer to this question is yes, then this is probably the right offer and you are very likely to convince them to volunteer their email. If your answer is no then you will need to think again. This really is one of the most important parts of this lead generation system and in order to create a really positive first experience with your prospect you need to really wow them with your offer.

## Create your landing page

Next you need to create a special landing page with your offer and your email opt-in capture form. You can either ask a web developer to create this for you or use a landing page generator service like, www.leadpages.com , www.launcheffect.com or www.instapage.com or www.unbounce.com . For a monthly fee these websites offer an incredibly user friendly service with numerous templates, design examples and tutorials to help you put your landing page together. Your landing page needs to be specific to the one goal you want to achieve which is to visually promote your offer and then capture the email addresses of your prospects.

## Create your thank you page

Most of the websites mentioned and your email service provider will offer you the opportunity to create a thank you page. Your thank you page is a great place to offer your subscribers the opportunity to share your promotion with their friends.

## Prepare your email campaign

You email list is one of the most valuable assets of your business and the main aim of your opt-in is to be able to communicate with your subscribers on an ongoing basis so that you can build trust, deliver valuable content and sell your products. If you craft your messages correctly you will be able to do all this without coming over as being pushy or over 'salesy'and continue to deliver content for years to come. If you haven't already done so then you will need to set up an account with an email service provider, for example, www.aweber.com or www.mailchimp.com or www.madmimi.com

## Create a compelling Facebook Post with your offer

To create your offer you simply need to create a post in your News feed by uploading a compelling image with an attention grabbing message.

- Upload a compelling image with an attention grabbing message on the image. ( Text must not take up anymore than 20% of the image)
- Add a compelling description of your offer. Starting your post with a question can be a very effective way of grabbing attention.
- Add your link to your special landing page.

## Select your audience

This is where Facebook really excels and you can really drill down and steer your campaign towards your exact target audience. Simply click on 'Boost Post' and you can target by demographics, interests and in advanced options you can target the fans of other pages as well.

## Go

Once your system is set up you are ready to push the button and go. It's really important to monitor your results at this stage to see what works and what does not. You may need to adjust your message, or offer, or graphic until you discover what really works. Once you have it right you have your very own system to create, capture and convert leads into customers and your very own brand advocates.

# How to Profit from Remarketing on Facebook

In today's digital world not do you have the opportunity to connect with your target audience through content and advertising you now have the opportunity to show off your products and services again to those people who have shown an interest by visiting our webpage but not actually taken the next step by signing up to an opt-in or buying our product or service. This is what is called remarketing and has to be one of the most powerful methods of marketing available to you today.

Even with opt-in and squeeze pages the fact is that the majority of people who land on your web page will disappear never to be seen again. There could be a number of factors or reasons why these browsers do not take any action:

- They are shopping around for the best deals.
- They are not in a right financial position to make the purchase at that time.
- They are distracted by a telephone call or something else.
- They have not heard of your brand before and are therefore unsure about your product.
- They are just not ready to make the buying decision.

Remarketing gives brands the opportunity to have another go at selling their products by showing adverts to the people who have previously visited their website.

Facebook allows their advertisers to create Custom Audiences from Facebook users who have taken a particular action on their website or mobile app. Advertisers can do this by adding a pixel code to their website and then delivering adverts relevant to the actions the users have already taken on the site. For example, a hotel booking website with the remarketing pixel added could be used to reach a group of people who have been searching for a hotel but never actually made the reservation. The advertiser could come back with an advert offering them a certain discount to tempt them back to make their reservation. A website offering a fashion range could come create an advert offering a discount to those people who had browsed their site but not purchased anything.

This remarketing is also a great way to have another go at getting users who have visited your website to sign up to your opt-in. For instance you could advertise your latest Webinar to those Facebook users who have already visited your website and since they have already visited your brands website they are more likely to sign up.

Facebook also allows you to create Custom Audiences from your current email list or your Mailchimp subscribers. To create Custom Audiences and use these features you will need to select 'Audiences' from the Adverts Manager menu and then select 'Create a Custom Audience'. You then need to select which audience you want to create and then agree to the terms and conditions. You can choose from:

- Data File Custom Audience
- Mailchimp Custom Audience
- Custom Audience from your Mobile App
- Custom Audience from your Website

When you choose the Website option you will need to add your Audience Name and Description and then select whether you want to include all website visitors or those who have visited specific pages only. You then need to set the time the people will be saved in your audience and lastly ask your developer to add the pixel code, supplied by Facebook, to your website.

# CHAPTER TEN

## *How to Win with Facebook's Algorithm*

FACEBOOK'S RECENT ALGORITHM has made it more difficult for businesses to reach their fans organically (without paying), and it does not look like it will change any time soon. However, there are very positive ways to look at this change, and there are many brands and pages that are doing very well and still receiving huge engagement without having to pay for it. Of course if you want to guarantee that all your fans see your posts then you will need to pay for it through Facebook's advertising reach, but there are ways that you can still reach your fans without paying.

One of the good things about this change is that it has cut out a great deal of unwanted noise. Therefore, users are seeing only what they really want to see in their News Feed and are not constantly being bombarded with posts that that they may not want to see. Facebook takes into consideration the posts that users are engaging with and will show more of these posts in their News Feed. Therefore, if you are creating valuable content that your audience is engaging with, you can actually gain more attention. Here are some tips on how to capitalize on Facebook's Algorithm:

- **Make every post count:** With every update, you need to make sure you stand out from the crowd by creating the best possible content. You also need to make sure that you put maximum thought into the way you craft and write your posts in order to receive the highest engagement. By focusing on engagement and encouraging your audience to comment, you are more likely to show up on their News Feed more often.

- **Create text only posts:** Even though image posts tend to get higher engagement, it is becoming evident that text posts are reaching more people in the News Feed. Asking questions is a great way to spark engagement.

- **Don't give up:** Many businesses are giving up and no longer posting updates, which is a huge opportunity for those who are sticking with it. So do continue posting. By staying the course and continuing to deliver high quality content to your audience, you are showing that you are in it for the long haul. If new people visit your page and see that you are no longer posting content, it's not going to do your brand any good.

- **Ask your audience to sign up:** Let your fans know that because of the new algorithm they are unlikely to see all your posts and, therefore, if they want to continue receiving valuable content, it's a good idea to sign up to your list.

- **Be realistic and set a budget:** If you have specific offers or things you want to say and you want to reach the majority of your fans and other targeted users, you are going to need to pay for it using Facebook's advertising platform. Therefore, be realistic, and if you believe Facebook advertising is a priority, work out how much you can afford to spend and set a budget for the year.

- **Promote your most valuable posts:** Make sure that the posts you promote are those that are going to be the most popular, so check how your post performs organically before you pay to promote it. You can usually tell within the first one to three hours how it is performing.

- **Let your fans know:** You can advise your fans that if they like your content and want to get your updates all the time then it would be a good idea to switch on **'Get Notifications'**. This is found by clicking the down arrow next to the 'like' button.

- **Value your fans:** Never has it been more important to show your fans how much you value them in a truly authentic way. Make sure that if your fans have taken the time to engage with your content that you engage with them and reward them by 'liking' their comments and commenting or answering their questions. If you do this, they are likely to come back again. If you a selling to businesses then make sure you reciprocate and share their content if it is relevant to your audience.

- **Create a group**: Creating a group around a topic which is of interest to your target audience can be an incredibly powerful way of promoting your brand and getting them to read your content and visit your blog.

- **Join Instagram:** You may find your fans are on Instagram as well, so if you haven't already gotten an Instagram account then this is the time to set one up. Instagram is a great way of reaching your fans organically, and you can post to both platforms at the same time.

# CHAPTER ELEVEN

## MEASURING AND MONITORING YOUR RESULTS ON FACEBOOK

MEASURING AND MONITORING your results and performance against your original goals and objectives on a continual basis is essential. This is where many businesses go wrong. They carry on aimlessly, posting content without checking to see what is working and what is not. Then after 6 months or a year, they wonder why their campaign is making no positive difference at all.

When you measure your results you will discover so much information about your campaign which will allow you to steer it in the right direction to achieve those SMART goals and objectives and stop anything that is not working.

When you originally work out your strategies and tactics for your campaign you will be estimating what you need to do to achieve your goals and objectives. However, as your campaign runs, you will see exactly what you need to do to achieve what you originally set out to do. For example, you may need to increase the amount you spend on advertising to attract new fans or you may need to change the types of posts you make to increase engagement and reach. Perhaps you need to increase the number of competitions you run to increase the number of opt-in subscribers. This is what it is all about. Make your campaign work for you by constantly measuring your success against the goals set and then adjusting your strategies accordingly in order to achieve the results.

You will easily be able to see the number of people who 'like' your page, the number of 'likes' you get for a post, or the number of opt-in subscribers. However, if you want to look at more detailed information, for example, the number of people Facebook is sending to your website or blog or how many of your Facebook fans are converting into customers, you will need to use Facebook Ads Manager, Facebook Insights, and Google Analytics. You can also use sites like Hootsuite and Buffer who provide analytics for Facebook.

## FACEBOOK INSIGHTS

Facebook **Insights** are found at the top of your page. Insights are a gold mine of information about how your campaign is performing, and it helps you monitor and understand what is and what is not working on your page and who is engaging with your posts. It also helps you make decisions about the best way to connect with your fans.

The insight layout has six tabs: overview, likes, reach, visits, posts, and people.

**The Overview Tab** shows what has been happening on your page in the last seven days and focuses on three metrics:
- **Page likes** - Total and new.
- **Page reach**- The total number of people who were shown your page and post.
- **Engagement** - The total number of unique people who engaged with your page as well as the type of engagement, 'likes' or comments. You will also see the last three posts that you created and how they performed.

**The Page Likes Tab** displays three metrics and shows you how your audience is growing:
- **Total Page** – 'Likes'.
- **Net Likes** – 'Likes' minus 'unlikes'.
- **Where your page 'likes' came from**

If you click on this graph it will show you why and how your 'likes' grew on your page on any day. This may be from ads or suggested pages, pages 'liked', posts by other pages, or by cellphone. You can also drag on the chart to display more than one day.

## The Reach Tab

- **Post Reach:** This shows you the number of people who saw your posts and how they saw them, either organic or paid. You can click on the chart to see more information about that day or drag on the chart to select more than one day and you can see what posts were being seen over that time. You can see positive engagement, 'likes', comments, and shares, and also negative information which shows if your post was hidden or whether a fan 'unliked' your page.

- **Total reach:** The total number of people who are shown any activity from your page, including posts from other people and check-ins.

## The Visits Tab

- **Page and Tab Visits:** The visits tab shows you a breakdown of where your visits are coming from.

- **Other Page Activity:** Shows you the number of actions people took that involved your page. This could be mentions, posts by other people on your page, offers purchased, and check-ins.

- **External Referrers:** Shows you the number of people who came to your page from outside sources, such as Google or Bing or other social sites etc.

## The Posts Tab

This tab is divided into two sections.

- **When your fans are online:** This shows you when the people who 'like' your page are on Facebook. You can put your mouse over a certain day and see when your fans are most likely to see your posts.

- **All posts published:** All posts published shows you all your posts in chronological order, how many people the post reached, and how they engaged and the actions that were taken ('likes', comments, or shares).

- **Post types:** Shows you average post performance based on reach and performance.

## The People Tab

- **Your fans:** This gives you demographic information about their age, gender, geography, and language. The age and gender chart shows how popular your page is with a certain age or gender compared to the total Facebook population.
- **People reached & people engaged:** These two tabs break down who has seen and engaged with your post by the same criteria.
- **People engaged**

## Check-ins

Soon to be introduced check-ins will show you information about who has checked in.

# FACEBOOK ADVERTS MANAGER

Your ads manager is where you can see at a glance how your campaigns are performing and analyze what is and what is not working. It's here that you can view your account and billing information, the number of post engagements, page 'likes', and your ad click through rates. You can also create ad reports. You can access your ads manager by clicking the 'gear' icon at the top of the page and then clicking **Manage Adverts**.

Your ads manager will show you comparisons between your different ads and how they are performing in terms of the number of clicks and the cost. When advertising, it's a really good idea to create quite a number of ads and change various aspects of the ad and then test each over a couple of days to see which are working best.

## Facebook Ads Reports

You can generate a number of reports with Facebook ads reports, and you can schedule these reports. You can set the frequency at which you want them created and then have them sent to your email address.

## Reports

Facebook lets you create and schedule reports in the ads manager. When you click on **Reports** you can then choose from General Metrics, Website Conversion, and Placement Reports:

- **General Metrics:** With this report you can select the time period you want to view and also customize the metrics so only you can see the information that is important to you.

- **Website Conversion:** This report lets you see how many conversions you received as a result of your Facebook ad. You do this with an offsite pixel, and you have to set up conversion tracking pixels on specific website pages to track specific conversions that happen on that page. To do this, go to your Ads manager, **Power Editor,** and then **Conversion Tracking** on the left side column. Give your conversion pixel a name and select a category from the drop down menu and then click **Create.** A pop-up box will appear where you can **View Pixel Code,** and this is the code you need to integrate into the page where you wish to track your conversions.

- **Placement Based Metrics:** This report shows the performance of your ad based on the placement of your ad and the devices your ad was shown on. For example, you can see the level of engagement for an ad in the News Feed from a cellphone or on the right side of Facebook on a desktop. With this report, you will be able to identify which type of device resulted in the highest engagement for your ad.

To view the information that is most important to you simply click on **Edit Columns** and use the column sets to view specific metrics you want to see in the report.

- **General**: Includes reach, frequency, impressions, amount spent, cost per impression (CPM), cost per click (CPC), clicks, click-through rate (CTR), and actions

- **Page**: Includes page 'likes', page engagement, offer claims, and cost per page 'likes'
- **Offsite**: Includes clicks, unique clicks, click through rate (CTR), link clicks, reach, impressions, amount spent, cost per click (CPC), and cost per impression (CPM)
- **App**: Includes app installs, app engagement, mobile app installs, and cost per mobile app installs
- **Conversion**: Includes conversions, checkouts, registrations, cost per website conversions, cost per checkout, and cost per registration
- **Demographic**: Includes your ad performance by age and gender
- **Geographic**: Includes your ad performance by country
- **Placement**: Includes performance broken down by placement, where your ad was shown on Facebook

## Old Reports

You can also create the following Old Reports:
- **Advertising performance:** This report includes statistics like impressions, clicks, click-through rate (CTR), and amount spent.
- **Responder demographics:** This report provides valuable demographic information about users who are clicking on your ads.
- **Actions by impression time:** This report shows the number of actions organized by the impression time of the Facebook Ad or Sponsored Story.
- **Inline Interactions:** This report helps you understand the engagement on page posts. It includes metrics like impressions, clicks, and detailed actions such as 'likes', photo views, and video plays that happened directly from your ads.
- **News Feed:** This report includes statistics about impressions, clicks, click-through rate (CTR), and average position of your ads and sponsored stories in News Feed. Use it to analyze the

performance of your ads and sponsored stories.

# GOOGLE ANALYTICS

In order to track the success of your campaign, it really is essential that you set up a Google Analytics account. With Google Analytics, you will easily be able to track how your campaign is performing in comparison to your other social campaigns, and Google Analytics will be able to give you detailed information about the impact Facebook is having on your business.

## Social Reports

Google Analytics provides advanced reports that let you track the effectiveness of your campaign with the following social reports:

- **The Overview Report:** This report lets you see at a glance how much conversion value is generated from social channels. It compares all conversions with those resulting from social media.

- **The Conversions Report:** The Conversions Report helps you to quantify the value of social media and shows conversion rates and the monetary value of conversions that occurred due to referrals from Facebook and any of the other social networks. Google Analytics can link visits from Facebook with the goals you have chosen and your E - commerce transactions. To do this you will need to configure your goals in Google Analytics, which is found under **Admin** and then **Goals**. Goals in Google Analytics lets you measure how often visitors take or complete a specific action, and you can either create goals from the templates offered or create your own custom goals. The Conversions report can be found in the **Standard Reporting** tab under Traffic Sources > Social > Conversions.

- **The Networks Referral Report:** The Networks Referral report tells you how many visitors the social networks have referred to your website and shows you how many page views and visits, the duration of the visits, and the average number of pages viewed per visit. From this information you can determine which network referred the highest quality of traffic.

- **Data Hub Activity:** The Data Hub Activity Report shows how people are engaging with your site on the social networks. You can see the most recent URL's that were shared, how they were shared, and what was said.

- **Social Plug-in Report:** The Social Plug-in Report will show you which articles are being shared and from which network. The Google + 1 button is tracked automatically within Google Analytics, but additional technical set-up is required for Facebook. Information about how to do this can be found on the Facebook Developers site.

- **The Social Visitors Flow Report:** This shows you the initial paths that your visitors took from social sites, through your site, and where they exited.

- **The Landing Pages Report:** This report shows you engagement metrics for each URL. These include page views, average visit duration, and pages viewed per visit.

- **The Trackbacks Report:** The Trackback report shows you which sites are linking to your content and how many visits those sites are sending to you. This can help you to work out which sort of content is the most successful so you can create similar content and also helps you to build relationships with those who are constantly linking to your content.

## Tracking Custom Campaigns with Google Analytics

Google Analytics lets you create URL's for custom campaigns for website tracking. This helps you to identify which content is the most effective in driving visitors to your website and landing pages. For instance, you may want to see which particular posts on Facebook are sending you the most traffic or you may want to see which links in an email or particular banners on your website are sending you the most traffic. Custom campaigns let you measure this and see what is and what is not working by letting you add parameters to the end of your URL.

You can either add you own or use the URL Builder.

To do this, simply type "URL builder" into Google and click on the first result. The URL builder form will only appear if you are signed into Google. You then need to add the URL that you want to track to the form provided, complete the fields, and click 'Submit.' You will then need to shorten the URL with bit.ly or goo.gl/ . Once you have set these up you can track the results within Google Analytics.

## MANAGING YOUR FACEBOOK CAMPAIGN

There are now numerous tools available on the Internet to help manage your campaign, particularly if you are using other networks to build your business. These will let you organize your multiple social platforms, see all your interaction in the same place, and also let you share your information across several social networks. Here are a few of the most popular, with information on the benefits you can offer.

### Hootsuite

Hootsuite is a social media management dashboard that helps you to manage and measure multiple social networks. You can manage up to five accounts for free, and it is designed so you can listen, engage, and manage all from one place. Hootsuite is Internet based, so there's no need to download any software. Other benefits include: scheduled tweets, bulk schedule with a csv file, and built-in analytics so you can measure your progress on multiple networks' social campaigns.

### Buffer

Buffer is a free online tool that lets you post to multiple accounts, including Facebook, LinkedIn, Twitter, and Google+, and schedule your updates. It offers automatic URL shortening and basic analytics. Buffer lets you post on your personal profiles as well as your business pages, and it also allows you to use bit.ly links so your followers will not know you are scheduling your tweets. Upgrading allows you to add more accounts and schedule more tweets than the basic free account.

## Socialoomph

Socialoomph has an impressive list of features to boost your social media productivity. Not only does it help you manage your Facebook, Twitter, and LinkedIn accounts, it also helps you schedule posts to your blog as well. There are free and premium options available.

# CHAPTER TWELVE

## BUILDING YOUR BRAND WITH FACEBOOK

YOUR MAIN AIM through this whole process is going to be to connect, capture, and convert your prospects through your website or blog, Facebook, and through other social networks, and this involves the following:

- **Connect:** Your product needs to be the connection between your prospect and what they need so the first thing you need to do is connect those two things. In order to do this you need to identify who they are, find them out of all the millions of people on the Internet, and then connect with them by offering them something they want or need.

- **Capture:** Once you have found them you need to capture them on your website, blog, Facebook, or any other social media platforms. This is so you can continue your relationship with them either by email or through Facebook and communicate your brand message. To do this you need to offer them some sort of incentive so you can capture their name and email address.

- **Convert:** When you have captured your prospect you need to convert them into a paying customer by nurturing them and continuing to build a relationship by offering them the content they want through email and Facebook and then moving them toward signing up for a special or exclusive offer.

To achieve this successfully you are going to need to have a well-defined brand, and that brand needs to be communicated through everything you do or say through Facebook, your website, blog, and your email campaign.

Whether you are a one person small business, a large corporation, or an organization, your brand is one of the most important attributes of your business. Your brand is what you want your prospects and customers to respect, trust, and fall in love with so they will buy and continue to buy your products and services. Your brand is what is going to set you apart from any other business and what will give your business the competitive edge.

Never has there been a better time for your business to build your brand and communicate your brand message to your target audience than through Facebook. Your brand is the main ingredient for success, and Facebook is giving you the channel to communicate it. You can literally communicate with your audience every day. If you get it right and connect the right brand experience with the right target audience, you are onto an all-around winner.

It may be that you have a well-established brand already or maybe you have not created your brand yet or it just needs some tweaking or fine tuning. Maybe you are not exactly sure what your brand is, or you feel it needs a complete overhaul. Whatever your situation is, you need to know that your brand is going to underpin your whole Facebook campaign, and it needs to be strong, clear, well-defined, and consistent. Once defined, your business is going to create it, be it, communicate it, display it, picture it, speak it, promote it, and most of all, be true to it. This chapter is going to take you through everything you need know and do to define and create your brand so you can get into the hearts and minds of your target audience by communicating the right message and brand experience.

There are many definitions of the word brand but this is the one I like best because it incorporates pretty much all the necessary information you will need to help you to define your own brand.

## Brand, the definition

Your brand is more than a name, symbol, or logo. It is your commitment and your promise to your customer. Your brand is the defined personality of either yourself as an individual brand or your product, service, company, or organization. It's what sets you apart and differentiates your business from your competition and any other business. Your brand is created and influenced by your vision and everything you stand for, including people, visuals, culture, style, perception, words, messages, PR, opinions, news media, and, especially, social media.

## Why is your brand so important to your business?

Branding is important because it helps you and your business build and create powerful and lasting relationships by communicating everything you want to say about your product or service to your prospects and customers. A strong brand encourages loyalty and will ultimately create a strong customer base and increase your sales by doing the following:

- Demonstrating to your prospects and customers that you are professional and committed to offering them what you promise
- Making your business easily recognizable
- Creating a clear distinction from your competition
- Making your business memorable
- Creating an emotional attachment with your audience
- Helping to create trust
- Helping to build customer loyalty and repeat custom
- Creating a valuable asset which will be financially beneficial if you sell your business
- Creating a competitive advantage

To do all the above you are going to have to find a way to get into the hearts and minds of your customers so they will ultimately buy and continue to buy your products or services. Before launching your campaign and setting up profiles, posting content, and engaging, you will need to have a clear picture of exactly what your brand is or what you want your brand to be. You will need to define exactly how your brand is perceived now, how you want your brand to be perceived, where your business fits into the market, who your target audience is, and how you want your business to develop in the future.

To do this you need a deep understanding of your business and the people who are going to be most interested in your products and how you are going to serve them. When it comes to defining your ideal target audience, you need to work out which of your products are the most popular and the most profitable so you can focus your efforts in finding and connecting with the right audience and then creating the right brand experience for them.

## YOUR VISION/YOUR STORY

If you want to create a strong brand, one of the first things you need to do is create a clear visual picture of how you see your business now and in the future. This is about daring to see what your business could be without constraints or limitations.

This exercise will not only help you work out what you want to achieve financially and creatively, but it also makes you focus on what really matters and will help you create your own unique voice and story. This is incredibly important when it comes to your branding as this is what is going to make your business stand out from others and give you that edge.

To do this, you need to get away from all distractions and think about how you would like to see your business grow and develop in the next three years. This is more than just putting a mission statement together. This is about your core business beliefs, why you are doing it, what you want your business to be, and how you want to be perceived in your market. To help you do this you will need to ask yourself the following questions and record your answers:
* Why did you originally start your business or why are you starting

a business?

- How did your original business idea come about?
- What changes are you looking to make in peoples' lives?
- What are you hoping to achieve?
- What aspects of your business are really important to you?
- What are your hopes and dreams?
- What is your definition of success?
- What sort of turnover and income defines that success?
- How many employees does your business have?
- Why are you in business?
- What are your core values in your business?
- What impact do you want to have?
- What influence do you want to have?
- What sort of things do you want the media to be saying about you?
- What do you want your customers to be saying about you?
- How you want to be portrayed on social media?
- How many Facebook fans do you want?
- What markets are you in? Are you local, national, or international?

Once you have completed this exercise, you will have all the material you need so that you can create the unique experience required to make your business stand out from all the others in your niche. This is the first step toward creating a brand for your business. This is the beginning of your story.

## DEFINING YOUR BRAND

Whether you are responsible for defining, creating, and developing your brand in-house or you are employing a local branding and marketing agency, you will need to carry out an analysis of your business to define your brand. Completing the following exercise will help you define and clarify your brand:

- A factual description of what your business is and the purpose of your business

- Describe your product or service in one sentence
- List all your products and/or services.
- What are the benefits and features of all of your products?
- Which are your most profitable products/services?
- Which are your most popular products/services?
- Who are your ideal customers for each of your products or services? (Consumer or business, age, gender, income, occupation, education, stage in family life cycle.)
- Out of these customers, which ones who are most likely to buy your most profitable products?
- Is the market and demand large enough to provide you with the number of customers you need to buy your most profitable products and achieve your financial goals?
- If your answer to the previous question is no then ask yourself the same question for each of your other products.
- Who are your three main competitors? (Have a look at their Facebook account.)
- What distinguishes your business from your competition? What special thing are you bringing to the market that is of real value? What is your unique selling point? What solutions are your products offering your customers that will meet their needs or solve their problems?
- If you are already in business, write down what your customers are already saying about your business. What do you think they would say about how your product or service makes them feel emotionally? (You may need to ask your customers if you do not already know.) What qualities and words would you use to describe the personality of your business as it is now? Here are some examples of words you may wish to use: high cost, low cost, high quality, value for money, expensive, cheap, excellent customer service, friendly, professional, happy, serious, innovative, eccentric, quiet, loud, beautiful, relaxing, motivating, sincere, adventurous, amusing, charming, decisive, kind, imaginative, proactive, intuitive, loving, trustworthy, extrovert,

vibrant, transparent, intelligent, creative, dynamic, resourceful.

- Now, whether you are already in business or starting out, write down all the words to describe how you want and need your brand to be perceived and what qualities you want to be associated with your brand in order to match the needs and expectations of your ideal customers. If you are already in business, hopefully this will be exactly the same as how you perceive you are at the current time.

- What is the evidence that backs up what you have said about your brand? This could be customer testimonials or any evidence about product or service quality.

- What is the biggest opportunity for your business right now?

- What products are you thinking of introducing in the near future?

## HOW TO GET INTO THE MINDS AND HEARTS OF YOUR TARGET AUDIENCE

Your target audience is your most important commodity, as they are the future customers and ambassadors of your business. Every single one of them is valuable, and every single one of them can make a difference to your business. This can be because they are actually going to buy your products or simply spread the word by interacting with you on Facebook.

However, it's a big social world out there. The possibilities of finding new people are limitless, but targeting everyone is not the solution. The biggest mistake you can make is trying to reach everyone and then not appealing to anyone. Your first step is to identify exactly who the people are who are going to be interested in your products or services, and then you need to find out everything about them. You need to get inside their heads and work out what motivates these people, what their needs, hopes, aspirations, fears, and dreams are. Your product or service is the link between them and what they want. When you know this you can tailor every single message or piece of content toward them.

When you know exactly who your ideal customers are, Facebook offers you the opportunity to go find and reach them. It's then up to you to capture them so you can continue to communicate. When you know everything about your customers you are more likely to speak the right language to be able to communicate with them and build trust to the point where the next natural progression is for them to buy your product.

It's only when you truly understand your audience that you can start converting them into customers. Once you know you are targeting the right audience, you can confidently focus every ounce of your effort creating exactly the right content, nurturing them, engaging with them, and looking after them. It's only a matter of time before they will buy your product.

## Creating your ideal customer persona or avatar

The following exercise is absolutely essential. Your answers to the questions will be the very information that is going to help you communicate with your customer in the right way, by providing them with the right content and the correct brand experience. Once you have done this exercise you are going to own some very powerful information. If you do not do this exercise it is very unlikely that you are going to be able to truly connect with your target audience in the way that is necessary to build trust so that you can ultimately convert them into your customers.

Your answers to the questions in the previous section will have given you a clear idea of which types of customers you need to target to give you the best chance of achieving your financial goals. You now need to find out everything about them so you can get your brand into their hearts and minds. The best way to do this is to create an imaginary persona or avatar of your ideal customer and you can build this picture by finding out the following:

- Describe your ideal customer and include the following details: are they a consumer or in business, their age, gender, income, occupation, education, and stage in family life cycle.

- Where do they live?
- What do they want most of all?
- What are their core values?
- What is their preferred lifestyle?
- What do they do on a day-to-day basis?
- What are their hopes and aspirations?
- What important truth matters to them?
- What motivates and inspires them?
- What sort of routines do they have?
- What are their day-to-day priorities?
- How do they have fun?
- What do they do in their spare time?
- What subjects are they interested in?
- Which books do they read?
- Which TV programs do they watch?
- What magazines do they read?
- Who do they follow on social media?
- Who are their role models?
- What really makes them tick?
- What are their fears and frustrations?
- What are their suspicions?
- What are their insecurities?
- What are their typical worries?
- What is the perfect solution to their worries?
- What are their dreams?
- What do they need to make them feel happy and fulfilled?

## Big Questions

To answer the following questions you will need to step inside your ideal customer's mind and imagine you are them.

- How do you feel when you find your product or service? What is your initial emotional reaction?
- What are the words that go through your head?

- How can I justify buying this product for myself?
- Are you ready to buy immediately?
- Do you have any suspicions that the product may not be what it says?
- What are those suspicions? Why do you have them?
- Do you need more convincing?
- What do you need to convince you that the product is right for you?
- What do you feel when you have the product in your hand?

The reason why these are such big questions is because your answers to them will establish whether or not you have correctly defined your ideal customer and whether you have really understood their needs, desires, and fears. If you are imagining yourself as your ideal customer and you are saying "woo-hoo", ecstatically jumping up and down with glee, immediately buying the product, or relieved that you have at long last found the solution to your problem, then you have created the right avatar. If not, then you need to think again.

It's only when you have imagined yourself in the hearts and minds of your target audience that you are going to be able to connect with them on any emotional level. With the information from the above exercise, you will have everything you need to produce exactly the right content to match the needs, desires, and expectations of your ideal customer so that you can create the right brand experience and sell your products. This information is like gold.

## COMMUNICATING YOUR BRAND

Once you have gone through all the processes outlined in this chapter you will have a clear idea about what your brand is, what is stands for, and how you stand out from similar businesses. You now have to work out how to best communicate this to your ideal customer so that when they hear or see your brand name they immediately make that essential emotional connection. This is what is going to make them eventually love your brand above all others.

When you are clear about what your brand is, what it stands for, and how you are going to stand out from other similar businesses, you then need to work out how you can communicate this message in the best possible way. Your main aim here is to create an emotional connection with your target audience that is going to help them grow to love your brand, remember your brand, and remain loyal to it. To do this you need to communicate your brand story through every aspect of your business, including your social media campaign.

With the information you now have you are armed with everything you need to create a consistent brand. If you have not already done so, you can either hand all this information over to a marketing agency or use it yourself to create all the following:

- **Your logo:** Your logo will give a clear guideline for all your promotional material, including your website or blog, stationery, templates, or any marketing material that needs to be created for online or offline promotion.
- **Your brand message: This is** the main message you want to communicate about your brand.
- **Your tagline:** A short, memorable statement about your brand that captures the personality of your brand and communicates how you or your product will benefit your customer.
- **All your 'about' descriptions:** You can communicate your brand story through all your 'about' sections on all your social media platforms you are using.
- **The content you create for your business:** Every piece of content you create for your business needs to be tailor-made for your target audience. You will need to pick who and what subjects or topics you want to be associated with your brand, as anything you pick to write about will be a representation of your brand.

- **Your website and/or blog:** The 'about' page of your website is probably the most visited page on any website and there is a reason for this. People want to find out about your business and what is different or special about it. This is a great place to introduce and expand on the story of your brand. This is where you can really go to town and communicate your beliefs and uniqueness.. Also, the visual style of your website or blog and your individual voice should be evident throughout your site and be consistent with your brand.

- **Video content:** Videos are an incredibly powerful way of creating a personal connection with your audience. Make sure that whatever video content you produce and whatever you say is always consistent with your brand.

# CHAPTER THIRTEEN

## *THE ESSENTIAL FACEBOOK MARKETING PLAN*

BEFORE LAUNCHING INTO your campaign you will need to know exactly what you want your business to achieve and what achieve and what you hope to gain through marketing on Facebook. Without the necessary planning and preparation, your campaign is very unlikely to succeed.

The next few chapters take you through everything you need to do to plan your campaign before actually posting content. In this chapter you will learn how to create your mission statement, set goals and objectives, and plan the strategies and tactics you need to implement to achieve those goals. In the following chapter you will learn exactly how to prepare your business, your website and blog, and your email campaign so you can capture and convert customers.

## *CREATING YOUR MISSION STATEMENT*

Many campaigns fail at the first hurdle simply because they do not have a clear idea about why they are undertaking a campaign or what they want to achieve. They set up a Facebook page and have little or no idea why exactly they are doing it. "Everyone else is doing it ... we probably should too." Then they launch in without first articulating the purpose of their Facebook campaign and aimlessly start posting content. Before long, they realize that this is having no positive effect on their business, and they either give up or continue half-heartedly.

Once you have defined your brand and your target audience you will need to produce your mission statement for your social media campaign. Your mission statement is vital for your business as a whole and for your prospects and customers, and it should clearly state your commitment and promise to them as well as communicate your brand message. You will be able to include this in your Facebook bio and on your business page. To create your mission statement, simply follow these for four easy steps:

- **Describe what your business does:** Describe exactly what you do, what you offer, and the purpose of your business.
- **Describe the way you operate:** Include your core values, your level of customer service, and your commitment to your customers. You can include how your core values contribute to the quality of your product or service.
- **Who are you doing it for?:** Who are your customers? Business owners, entrepreneurs, working women, gardeners, shop owners, etc.
- **The value you are bringing:** What benefit are you offering your customers ? What value are you bringing them?

Once you have created your statement, everyone will know exactly what you are about. You will know what you need to deliver to your customers. Your employees will know what is expected of them. Your customers and prospects will know what your promise is and what they can expect when buying your products and services.

## SETTING YOUR GOALS AND OBJECTIVE FOR YOUR FACEBOOK CAMPAIGN

Setting goals and objectives is the key to your success on Facebook. Once they are set, you will be ready to plan and create the strategies and tactics to achieve those goals and objectives. You will be able to review and measure the success of your campaign.

# Definition of a goal

A goal is a statement rooted in your business's mission, and it will define what you want to accomplish and offer a broad direction for your business to follow. The three main goals of any business will ultimately be to increase sales, to reduce costs, and to improve customer service. Each goal will have a direct effect on the others. Here are some examples within those three main goals:

## 1. To increase revenue and generate sales

- To increase website traffic
- To increase brand awareness through Facebook
- To build a reputation as an expert within the industry
- To build a loyal and engaged community on Facebook
- To increase the number of customers from word-of-mouth and referrals
- To increase the number of sales
- To increase average spending per customer
- To increase the number of leads generated
- To introduce new products
- To increase online visibility
- To promote an event
- To build a highly targeted list of email subscribers
- To connect with new customers
- To build trust and build relationships with prospects and customers
- To put a content marketing strategy in place
- To increase business in 'X' country/state
- To become a thought leader in your industry
- To develop new markets by introducing product into 'X' country/state
- To decrease spending on traditional forms of advertising and invest 'X' amount in Facebook marketing
- To build relationships with key influencers on Facebook

## 2. To reduce Costs

- To decrease spending on traditional forms of advertising and invest in Facebook marketing

## 3. To deliver customer satisfaction and retain customers

- To answer customer questions promptly
- To respond to customer complaints promptly, politely, and helpfully
- To provide online help/technical support
- To respond to customer feedback
- To listen to your customers

## Setting measurable objectives

Once you set your broader goals, you need to get more specific and create SMART objectives (specific, measurable, attainable, relevant, and timely). Here is an explanation of exactly what each of those terms means:

- **Specific:** You need to target particular areas for improvement.
- **Measurable:** Your progress needs to be quantifiable, and putting concrete figures on your goals is essential for success and is the only way to measure the effectiveness of your campaign.
- **Attainable/Realistic:** You need to be realistic with the resources you have available, and the results you are expecting need to be realistic.
- **Relevant:** Your goals need to be relevant to the business climate you are in.
- **Time Bound:** Make sure you set a realistic time period to achieve your goals. If a time is not set then things tend not to get done.

Here are some examples of the sort of SMART objectives you should be setting:

- Increase sales of product X by X%
- To build an audience of X number fans on Facebook within one year.
- To increase number of followers by X per week
- To increase website traffic from Facebook by X times
- To increase opt-in list subscribers by X per week
- Increase conversions from Facebook by X per week
- To increase the number of leads generated from Facebook by X per week
- To increase the number of new customers by X per month
- To increase the average spending per customer by X
- Introduce X number of new products every 6 months
- To increase sales from X country/state by X%
- To decrease spending on traditional forms of advertising by X and invest X amount in Facebook marketing
- To achieve a X% reach (number of people who see posts) on Facebook
- Utilize Facebook to increase attendants at X event by X people
- Utilize Facebook to increase YouTube views by X people per week

## CHOOSING YOUR STRATEGIES AND TACTICS

Once you have set your quantifiable goals and objectives, you are going to have to work out how you are going to accomplish them through Facebook. You will need to think about the strategies and tactics you are going to use, and they need to be quantifiable as well. Here are some examples of the strategies you may want to implement:

- To create a free offer with built-in subscriber opt-in form
- To post content on Facebook X times per day
- To make X% of posts photo/posts
- To spend X on promoted posts per month
- To create X number of highlighted posts per month
- To spend X on Facebook advertising

- To increase spend on Facebook advertising in X country/state by X%
- To create X number of blog posts per week/month and post them on Facebook with images
- To post X offers per month/6 months on Facebook
- To run X competitions/contests per year on Facebook
- To create X events on Facebook
- To create X videos on YouTube per month
- To spend X minutes per day liking customers pages (B2B only)
- To spend X minutes per day 'liking', commenting, and sharing customer posts
- To follow X influencers on Facebook per week
- To create X number of online events per year

Of course, at the beginning, you are going to need to make an educated guess at the number of times you need to do one thing to achieve another. As your campaign runs, you will need to adjust certain aspects to achieve your goals. For example, you may need to spend more on promoted posts to increase your reach, spend more advertising to increase the number of fans, or you may need to change the type of content you are posting to increase the amount of engagement.

The only way you can do this is by constantly monitoring and measuring your results against the original goals and objectives you set and adjusting your campaign accordingly.

## CREATING YOUR FACEBOOK POSTING CALENDAR

Now that you have your strategies in place, you will have a good idea of the amount and type of content you need to post to achieve those objectives. One of the most challenging tasks of your Facebook campaign is going to be to consistently deliver a high standard of content to your fans on a daily basis. You are going to need to post between one to four times a day. This does not mean you need to create numerous blog articles each day, but you are going to need to communicate in some way and find unique ways for your audience to interact with your brand and offer some kind of value on a regular basis. This may seem daunting to begin with, but you will be surprised just how one idea leads to another.

To help you map out your content for the next six months or the year ahead, you need to create a Facebook posting calendar which is going to be your key to consistent posting. There are many online tools and apps that can help you with this. Google Calendar is a very good calendar to use, and it lets you color code the different types of posts. You can also use Hootsuite, the social media dashboard, to plot out your calendar or use a spreadsheet in Excel. There are also other online applications, like www.trello.com, which has easy to use drag-and-drop features. Using mind-mapping applications like 'Simplemind' can really help when brainstorming for content ideas.

To get started you will simply need to map out and schedule the days of the week for each week of the year and decide what types of post you are going to create for certain days. You will need to balance the type of content in order to create variety and interest for your audience. You then need to create topics or themes and break the year down into weeks/months and make a schedule. You can add all the things that you are planning within your business, like offers, contests, product launches, and webinars, and then add all the things going on outside your business, like public holidays and special events. You need to incorporate all that information into your daily action plan.

It may seem daunting to look at a blank calendar, but you will be surprised how it comes together when you start breaking it down into months, weeks, and days. A posting calendar will help you keep your campaign focused, on track, and in line with your brand and your marketing goals and also keep it balanced in terms of the subject and type of media you use. A calendar will help you look ahead and help you to incorporate your marketing plan into your Facebook campaign. It may be that you are launching a new product, or maybe certain products tie in with specific holidays. You may have certain industry events you need to attend or are perhaps creating your own. Maybe you are going to run a competition at a certain time of the year. Whatever it is you are planning throughout the year, you need to include it on your calendar.

The following example shows how by creating a regular weekly schedule you can really simplify the process of creating your social media posting calendar:

## Week 1
**Monday**
**AM**        Inspirational quote image to start the week
**PM**        Post a useful tip
**Special**   Post a competition teaser

**Tuesday**
**AM**        Link to weekly blog post with image
**PM**        "Caption this photo"

**Wednesday**
**AM**        Post a cartoon that relates to your niche
**PM**        "Fill in the blank" post

**Thursday**
**AM**        Post an engaging question which is business related (B2B)
**PM**        Post or share an infographic (B2B)
**Special**   Post contest photo and entry details

**Friday**
**AM**        Share a business tip (B2B)
**PM**        Post a weekend photo wishing all a happy weekend
**Special**   Holiday weekend post

**Saturday**

**AM**   Post a question that is not business related

**Sunday**

**AM**   Share a funny video

**PM**   Post a relaxing image for a Sunday

This is just an example and you obviously need to tailor this to your business with the content that is important to your particular target audience and the frequency at which you want to post that content.

# CHAPTER FOURTEEN

## PREPARING YOUR BUSINESS FOR SUCCESS

WHETHER YOUR SITE is being found through an organic search, an advertising campaign, Facebook, or any other social media platform, all your hard work is going to be wasted unless you have put a system in place to capture leads and convert them into customers. This system has to start from the moment your prospect either hits your website, your blog, or your Facebook page, and your ultimate goal is to convert your browsers into buyers.

Firstly, the unfortunate fact is that the majority of your website visitors are unlikely to buy from you on their first visit. If you do not have a website that grabs their attention within the first couple of seconds, they will move very quickly onto another site. Secondly, even if your site does catch their eye, they are still likely to check out other sites and still may not return. To make any kind of impact at all your site needs to grab their attention and then capture their email address so you can continue your relationship with them through email. This chapter is going to take you through steps you will need to take, from getting your website or blog ready to setting up and creating your email campaign.

Email is still one of the most powerful ways to convert prospects into customers and has a conversion rate three times higher than social media conversion rates. That is not to say that your Facebook campaign is any less important, as this is where you are going to find and nurture your leads and transfer them to your opt-in by either capturing them on Facebook or on your website or blog. This chapter is going to take you through steps you will need to take from getting your website or blog ready to setting up and creating your email campaign.

## PREPARING YOUR WEBSITE FOR SUCCESS

Whether you already have a website or blog or you are creating a new site from scratch, you need to make sure it has the necessary features to grab the attention of your target audience and capture their email addresses. Capturing the email addresses of your target audience has to be one of your most important goals when creating your website. Once your prospects have voluntarily submitted their email address, you have the opportunity to build a relationship, communicate your message, and promote your products and services on an ongoing and regular basis. A well thought-out and crafted email campaign can immediately establish trust and favor with your subscribers. Don't forget that it is you who owns your opt-in list and nobody can take it away from you. As long as you are providing your subscribers value with great content, they are likely to want to keep hearing from you. Remember you cannot rely on social media to continue your relationship as these platforms are changing all the time. You need to build your email list.

Once you have completed the exercise in the branding section and have your ideal customer persona or avatar, you will have a clear picture of what your target audience's pain point or problem is and how your product can help solve it or make their life better in some way. If you have a blog, and most businesses today need a blog, you will also have all the tools you need to create the right content to attract your target audience. Armed with this information you are halfway ready to putting a system in place, so your products sell themselves and your website is working like an extra sales person selling your products 24/7.

When your visitor arrives at your site, you have only three seconds to grab their attention. You need to connect emotionally with them and let them know immediately that they have arrived at the right place by communicating exactly how you are going to help them and what it is you are offering them.

Once they are on your site, you then need to win their interest and confidence so that they will voluntarily submit their email address. To do this you will need to create a lead magnet and offer your audience something which is incredibly valuable to them for free. There are numerous ways you can do this and which one you use will depend very much on what type of business you are and what your goals are. If you are a business offering technical solutions, you could offer them a free trial. If you are offering information, you could offer them a free report, a short video training series, or an ebook. If you are selling some kind of product or service, you could offer them a money-off voucher. These work particularly well for restaurants and the service industry as a whole. Whatever you are offering, it needs to be really good to attract your audience and get them to volunteer their email.

Here are the features you need to have on your website or blog or any landing page with a special offer.

- **Keep your design simple:** Your site needs to have a clean and simple design, and you need to communicate your most important message clearly and concisely to your target audience. Your most important content with any call-to-action needs to be placed above the fold, where they will be easily seen, and your call-to-action should have an easily seen button link rather than just a text link.
- **Make your site easy to navigate:** Really this is so important. Try to use the minimum number of pages you can and make your menu titles as easy to understand as possible.
- **Clearly communicate your message:** You want your visitors to subscribe to your opt-in, so you need to place your compelling offer with an image and title of the offer someplace where it is visible. The message and benefit of your offer needs be descriptive and specific.
- **Add a clear call-to-action:** In order for your visitors to sign up,

they will need to be told what to do. Make sure you have a direct call-to-action, for example, "Download your free ebook now" or "Sign up for your discount voucher now." Your call-to-action needs to be clearly visible with an eye-catching button link which is much more effective than a text link.

- **Add clear contact information:** Make it easy for your prospects to contact you by placing your contact details where they will be easily seen. With the technology available, you can even add chat features so that as soon as your prospect arrives on your site a chat form appears asking if you can be of any assistance. Obviously you need the resources to be able to man this, but it is an incredibly powerful way of quickly building trust and showing how much you value your website visitors by being available to answer any of their questions.

- **Email capture form:** Your email capture form needs to be as simple as possible, preferably just asking for their name and email. You need to state on the form that their email address is safe with you and will not be shared with anyone. Make sure your form is in a prominent position and consider using a pop-up form that appears 20 seconds after your prospect has arrived on your site. Your email sign-up form needs to go at the top, side, and bottom of your webpage and also on your 'about page,' which is often the most popular page on your site.

- **Privacy policy:** You need a clear privacy policy on your website to make it clear that you will not be spamming them or selling their information.

- **Thank you page:** Once your visitor has completed the form, you will have them as a lead, but before you let them go you can send them to a thank you page where you can offer them the opportunity to share your offer with their friends by including social sharing buttons.

- **Mobile Friendly:** You need to make sure your offer is easily visible and easy to complete on a cellphone. This is incredibly important, as more and more people are purchasing from their cellphone. There is nothing more annoying for the user than if the site is hard to navigate from their cellphone.

- Don't add external links to other sites. Be careful not to fall into the trap of wanting to make your site more interesting by adding lots of content and links to other external sites, as this will only detract from your main goals and you'll end up sending traffic away from your site.

## Landing pages

Landing pages are incredibly effective if you want to promote specific offers for specific products to specific audiences. A landing page is a page that is designed to give information about an offer and then capture a lead with a form for your visitor to complete so that they can download or claim that offer. Landing pages are highly effective in capturing leads because they are designed to be specific in their goal, which is to capture the contact information of your visitor.

The landing page should have a clear, uncluttered design and not have any links or navigation menus that could take your visitor away from the landing page. It should contain the following:

- A headline (The title of the offer)
- A description of the offer, clearly detailing the benefits to your visitor
- A compelling image of the offer
- A clear call-to-action. This can be in the form of an image or text.
- A form to capture contact information (The fewer fields required to be completed, the more leads you will receive.)
- A clear privacy policy on your website that makes it clear that you will not be spamming them or selling their information
- A thank you page leading them to another offer or social sharing

You can either ask your web developer to create landing pages or there are numerous tools available on the Internet where you can easily create one, for example: www.leadpages.net, www.unbounce.com, www.launcheffect.com, and www.instapage.com

## SETTING UP AND CREATING YOUR EMAIL CAMPAIGN

Once you have created your lead capture system on your website, blog, or separate landing page and have your subscribers' permission to send them your email, you are going to need a really good email campaign to convert those leads into sales.

Email is still one of the most effective forms of converting leads into sales, and email is more powerful than ever. Not only is it cost effective but it also provides one of the most direct and personal lines of communication with your customer. Once subscribed, they have invited you into their inbox on a regular basis and producing valuable content for your subscribers will develop trust and deepen your relationship with them. Your email will also work hand in hand with your Facebook campaign. As you build your relationship with your fans on Facebook, they are more likely to deem your emails valuable and open them.

The first thing you need to do is set yourself up with a good email marketing provider and there are many you can choose from: www.aweber.com, www.constantcontact.com, and www.mailchimp.com to name a few. It's important to use a system where you have a confirmed opt-in. This is when the subscriber is sent an email to confirm their email address. This verifies that you are gaining consent and legally protects you. It also helps you to keep a clean list, and it protects you from sending emails to incorrect addresses. You can then automate your emails with an auto responder and send out emails automatically over time.

Your next task is to plan and create your email campaign. Here are a few tips for doing so:

- **Be clear about your goals:** You need to be absolutely clear from day one what you want to achieve through email. Are you using it to introduce a new product at some time? Are you launching an event? Whatever you do, make sure you know exactly what it is that you want to achieve.

- **Keep it simple and in line with your branding:** Make sure your email design ties in with your branding. Most email providers offer templates which you can add your own branding to, or you can get a designer to create a particular design. Keep it really simple. Sometimes if things are too fancy they become impersonal.

- **Send a regular newsletter:** Plan to send a regular newsletter email at least once a month and once a week if you can. You can also plan to send off information about offers which tie in with special holidays and occasions throughout the year or competitions or events that you may be planning.

- **Plan your topics:** You need to plan the topics you want to cover in each email, and this should tie in nicely with the plan for your blog articles. You then need to deliver high quality content which is tailor-made to fit with your subscribers' interests, and it needs to be so good that they are looking forward to the next email from you. If you are sending emails about offers then you need to show them clearly how these offers are going to benefit their lives.

- **Attention-grabbing titles:** This is where you need to get really creative. Your main goal here is to get your subscriber to open your email, and you need to create a headline that is going to make your subscriber curious and inquisitive and eager to open your mail. Questions work really well as titles, and you will often see your open rates increase. This is because people find questions intriguing and they feel like you are directly addressing them. Try and avoid the words that will trigger spam filters. Simply search Google for a list of these words to avoid.

- **Be authentic and true to your brand:** Write your emails in a style that your audience will grow to recognize, 'like,' and identify with your brand. Write so your subscriber feels like you are just writing to them. You need to establish yourself as a likeable expert for your subscribers. Try and create a personal relationship with them by addressing them by name and giving them a warm friendly introduction. Offering them the opportunity to connect with you and answer any of their questions by simply replying to your mail is a great way to create a connection and trust.

- **Keep it simple** Make sure your emails are simply constructed and straight to the point so you keep your subscribers' interest and get them quickly to the place you want them to go, like your blog or offer.

- **Include social sharing buttons:** Include all your social sharing icons and links in your mail.

- **Make them feel safe:** Make sure your subscribers are clear that their email will not be shared and that they can unsubscribe anytime.

- **Analyze your open rates:** Most email service providers include statistics in their packages so you can analyze open rates, bounce rates, click through rates, unsubscribers, and social sharing statistics. These results give you the opportunity to find out what is and what is not working.

## CHAPTER FIFTEEN

## *BLOG BLOG BLOG*

THIS CHAPTER IS for anyone who does not have a blog. The word blog has been mentioned numerous times throughout the book and has become an essential part of any online business today.

## *WHAT IS A BLOG?*

A blog (short for web log) is a term used to describe a website that provides an ongoing journal of individual news stories which are based around a certain subject or subjects (blog posts.) Blogs have given people the power of the media. Anyone can now create a personal type of news that appeals to a high number of small niche audiences.

Bloggers simply complete a simple online form with a title and body and then post it. The Blog post then appears at the top of the website as the most recent article. Over time the posts build up to become a collection of posts which are then archived chronologically for easy reference. Each blog post can then become a discussion with space for comments below the post, readers can leave comments and questions. This is where bloggers start to build relationships and a community with their readers and other bloggers who may have similar interests. Blogs were one of the earliest forms of social media and started growing in the late 1990s. The number of blogs has exploded in recent years and blogs now underpin the majority of successful social media campaigns.

## *WHY BLOG FOR BUSINESS?*

Blogging is one of the most beneficial tools that a business has to communicate it's expertise and ideas to its prospects and customers and to engage with them. Businesses can share information about their business and about any subject that may be of interest to their niche. It is a fact that businesses with blogs benefit from an increase in the number of visitors to their website, increased leads, increase in inbound links and increased sales. Here are some of the reasons why and the benefits that come with blogging:

- **Underpins your whole social media campaign** Your blog is the focus of all your social media efforts and the centre of all your content marketing efforts. One of the main goals of any business today will be to get people to their blog to read their valuable and targeted content and social media will be one of the main tools they can use to drive traffic to their blog.

- **Increased website traffic** A well optimised blog will increase your chances of being found in search. Google loves unique fresh content and if this is created regularly, this will boost your traffic.

- **Builds brand awareness** A Blog offers a business the opportunity to build a community and build awareness for their products or services. The more people who see your blog, the more people see your brand.

- **Provides valuable information for your niche** Creating a Blog gives your business a voice and provides your niche with valuable information in relation to the subjects that they are interested in. This may include information about market trends, industry news and insight into your products and services and what is behind them.

- **Thought leadership** Sharing your expertise with valuable information will make you stand out as a thought leader in your particular field and will help you to build a professional online reputation.

- **Builds trust & creates warm leads** When you are providing valuable content for your niche on a regular basis, answering their questions and addressing their concerns, this in turn creates trust between you and your prospective customers. This trust leads to more leads and will result in sales. When your audience become regular readers of your blog they become warm rather than cold leads, the ice has been broken and they are half way there in terms of buying your product.

- **You gain more knowledge** While writing your blog you will be continually researching your subject, learning about new technology, products and new trends. In turn, this keeps you ahead of the game and in the eyes of your customers it makes you an expert. As time goes by you become more and more knowledgable and can steer your business in line with market trends and keep your products and services up to the minute. You will also find that blogging is inspiring and your ideas will snowball, as you learn more material you will find more material to blog about.

- **Interaction and feedback** When your blog has room for comments and discussion it will give you the opportunity to hear what people are saying, the questions they are asking and insight into what they want out of your products. Feedback like this is invaluable to your business and also leads to more ideas for more blog posts. This kind of feedback also encourages a conversation and you actually get the opportunity to communicate with prospective customers.

## HOW TO CREATE A BLOG?

Creating your blog is incredibly straight forward. There are a number of free blogging platforms that are available, however, if you read the terms and conditions of most of these platforms you will find that at the end of the day you do not actually own the content and you will not have full control of your blog. You will have no control of the advertising displayed, you are unlikely to be able to include an email capture form, you will not be able to have you own domain name and you will not be able to install plugins. With a free platform your domain name will look something like http://mybusinessblog.theirblogplatformname.com and overall it is not going to look that professional.

The best and safest way of creating a blog and running with your own domain name is to create one with wordpress.org or you can use website creators like www.wix.com or www.squarespace.com who both offer blogs with their product and you can add your own domain. Using any of these will give you full control over your site.

Wordpress.org is a free open source platform which means it can be modified and customised and by anyone. You can use custom themes or you can choose from hundreds of free themes and plugins. The wordpress.org blogging platform is free but you will need to purchase a domain name and host your site on your own server, however most hosting companies offer inexpensive monthly plans and a one click installation solutions. You will also need to make sure you back up your blog and you may very well find this is included in your hosting package.

## What Makes a Successful Blog?

For those businesses that are doing it right blogging can be hugely beneficial and they will often see an increase of over 50% of website visitors and leads. However, many blogs also fail to make any positive difference to a business, so it is essential that before you waste time and resources you understand what you need to do to create a successful blog:

### Set Goals and objectives

First of all you will need to be about clear what your marketing goals are and set clear objectives for what you want to achieve from your blog.

### Example Goal 1

Increase brand awareness through Facebook.

### Objective:

Achieve X number of shares per month on Facebook.

## Example Goal 2
Increase Traffic to website from blog.
**Objective:** To achieve an increase of X Traffic from blog.

## Example Goal 3
Increase the number of leads for product A.
**Objective:** To gain X number of new opt-ins per week.

## Example Goal 4
To create interaction and engagement.
**Objective:** To have at least X number of comments on each blog post.

## Example Goal 5
To become a thought leader in the industry.
**Objective:** To write X number of guest posts per month/year.

## Example Goal 6
To increase the ranking of blog in Google and Bing.
**Objective:** To achieve X number of backlinks from other websites in 6 months.

## Create top content for your audience
Again it's all about your audience and what they want, what they are interested in, what makes them tick and what problems they need solving. If you can identify these things then you are half way to finding the valuable content that is going to keep your audience interested and engaged. When you create your content it needs to be either inspiring, educational, informative or entertaining. If you can create content that people really value, they are more likely to share your content, more likely to sign up for your updates and more likely to come back looking for more. Creating content around your product or services is not going to provide enough interest to your readers and it is unlikely to get shared. Of course the occasional post is ok but try and keep away from this unless you can tie it in with something which is of real value to your

audience.

## Create a content plan

Your content plan is the backbone to your blog. You will need to decide what topics you are going to build your blog around so that you can stay consistent. There may be certain keywords that you want to target and need to incorporate into your content. Once you know your topics or subjects then you can decide which types of posts you are going to create. There are numerous types of blog posts you can use, for example; tutorials, how to's , interviews, reviews, book reviews, advice, Q and A's, case studies, trend reports and the latest news in your industry. When you have decided on all this you then write a schedule and if you have certain events that happen every year in your industry make sure you include these in your plan.

## Newsworthy posts

Make sure you are blogging about whats new in your industry and keep an eye on trending topics relating to your industry so you can create blog posts that are really up to date. You can do this by checking out what is trending on the social sites and also signing up for Google alerts which will keep you up to date on new info relating to your interests and queries.

## Frequent and consistent blogging

It is proven that the more high quality content you produce, the more views your blog will get. You will need to post at least once a week if not more. Google loves fresh content so the more posts you have, the more opportunities you are going to have to be found.

## Optimise your blog for search

Look for keywords and phrases that people are looking for. There are tools available to do this like word tracker, Google trends and Google keyword planner. You can find out the amount of competition by typing a phrase into Google search and seeing how many results it brings up. In order to get found you will need to concentrate your efforts on low competition keywords and phrases and the more specific your words and phrases are the better. You can then create your content around your chosen keyword or phrase as long as the content is highly relevant. When creating your blog post make sure you put the word/phrase in the page title, the header and the body. If you put the phrase in your meta tag it will be displayed in bold font in the search results which will make it stand out even more.

## Attention grabbing headline

To catch your readers attention you need a good headline, a headline that will need to intrigue your audience enough to make them feel that they absolutely have to read this post. It needs to be simple and to the point as well as containing valuable keywords. Here are some example headlines that really work:

How to .......

7 ways to successfully .........

Why you should do ..... to .......

Secrets that every ...... should know.

The secret formula for success in ......

5 quick and easy ways to .........

What every serious ...... should know about......

7 things every ..... should avoid to ......

## A great design

Your blog needs to be inviting and although the content is what people are looking for the blog still needs to be visually appealing and reflect your brand. If your blog is just text based it's going to look cold and uninviting and lack interest, so you need to include compelling images to engage your audience. It is definitely a good idea to spend time researching different themes. Another thing to watch with your design is your side bar, make sure you have only what is absolutely necessary so you do not pull your readers attention away from the action you want them to take.

## Formatting

You need to make it as easy as possible for your reader to read and digest your blog. If you format your blog with headings, bold subtitles and bullet points it will be a much more enjoyable to read than one long paragraph.

## Ask a question at the end of your post

Asking a question at the end of your post is likely to provoke discussion. People like to think their opinions matter and it's a great way for your readers to interact and network with each other too. Make sure you answer any questions your readers ask, there is nothing worse than seeing bloggers ignoring their readers.

## Tags

Tags help people to find your content within your blog and with the search engines, they also help to group related posts together.

## 11 THINGS EVERY BLOG SHOULD HAVE

### An incentive to join your opt-in

One of the main goals of your blog is to captures leads. The majority of your readers will probably only read one of your blog posts so it's really important to try and get them on your opt-in list so they will keep reading your blog. You will need to make sure you give them some kind of incentive to complete the email capture form, like a free report, free ebook, or simply email updates.

### An engaging image

A blog needs at least one image to make it look interesting and inviting. Blogs without images are simply boring. You can use your own images, stock photos, or images from photo sharing sites like Flickr.

### Clear call-to-actions

You need to make it very clear both within and outside of your text. what you want your readers to do. This could be anything from signing up for email updates, a free trial, a free offer, a request for a quote, or more information on a product.

## Email capture form

You can either include a prominent form on your blog or install a pop-up mail capture form. If you do install a pop-up then make sure the reader has a good few seconds to read the heading and start reading the article before the form pops up. It is also a good practice to put at least three email sign-up forms on the page, one below the article, one in the footer, and one on the top beside the article or right above it.

## About section

Your "about" section is the introduction to you and your blog. It's probably the most viewed page of any blog. People like to know who is writing the blog and feel acquainted with that person, so you need to get your personality over in this section. Make sure you include your name and a picture of yourself. This will help your readers make a personal connection with you. A video of yourself is also a great a way of getting your readers acquainted too. Above all, focus on how you are going to help your readers, what problems you are going to solve for them, and introduce some of the topics you are going to talk about. Remember, your blog is about your audience's needs and not yours.

## Contact page

A simple contact form works best but also make it really easy for people to reach out to you. Make sure you include all your social sharing buttons and an email capture form.

## Easy to search archives

If the content of your blog posts is interesting your readers are going to want to read more so you need to make the previous blog posts easily accessible. On many sites it really is incredibly difficult to find content, so you need to get yourself a custom archive page. A search box at the top of your blog is a great idea for helping your readers find content.

## Social sharing plug-ins

You need to include buttons or links to all the social networks where you have a presence. There are hundreds of plug-ins you can use to do this. Also make sure you have sharing buttons next to your articles as well.

## RSS Feed

RSS (Rich Site Summary) is a format for delivering regularly changing content on the Internet. It saves you from checking the sites you are interested in for new content. Instead, it retrieves the content from sites you are interested in. Make sure you have the RSS feed and then have a clear call-to-action making it clear why they should subscribe to your feed. If you want to keep up-to-date with your favorite bloggers you can sign up to either My Yahoo, www.bloglines.com, or www.newsgator.com.

## Comments section

Your blog needs a comment section which will encourage interaction and help you to build relationships with your readers. You can install Facebook comments easily with a WordPress plug-in. Disqus is another favorite comment provider.

## A guest bloggers welcome page

Guest posting is becoming more and more important in the blogging community and making it obvious that you will accept guest posts is going to go a long way to building relationships with other bloggers. The benefits of having other people contributing to your blog are that you will have more valuable content on your site and more exposure if your guest blogger promotes their posts on their site. You may also gain from the opportunity to produce a guest post on their blog at a later date. Guest blogging is a top method of getting back links to your blog, which is essential for search engine optimization.

### Privacy policy & terms of service pages

Make it clear your email readers are safe with you and you are not going to share their information with any other parties.

## PROMOTING YOUR BLOG

If you want to run a successful blog, you cannot just rely on search to get it out into the blogosphere. You need to find other ways of promoting your content and getting found.

- **Promote on your social sites:** Posting your blog content on social sites is essential. You can connect your blog to Twitter and Facebook so your content is automatically shared. Or you can use Hootsuite or Tweetdec to share your content to multiple sites, which will save you time. When posting, use an image to grab your audience's attention and make sure you use popular hashtags for your topic which will open up more opportunities to being found by new people.

- **Guest blogging:** Guest blogging is a great way of gaining a larger following. It will also give your blog more exposure, credibility, and increase your inbound links, which is essential for SEO. Most bloggers allow guest bloggers to post their bio, including their social profiles and blog URL, on their site.

- **Social sharing buttons:** As mentioned previously, it is essential to have social sharing buttons next to your blog articles.

- **Comment on other blogs:** There is so much opportunity for you to promote yourself today with the number of blogs and social sites. If you comment on other peoples' blogs you can often leave a URL, but only if it is relevant to the article being commented on and you are adding some value to the article.

- **Website and email:** If you have a website then try and point people to your blog. You can do this by adding visual links on your "about" page and other pages. Also make sure you have a link to your blog in your email and send an email to your current contacts telling them about your blog.

- **Create a Google Adwords campaign:** If you are serious about driving traffic to your site and generating leads and you have your blog set up to catch leads and subscribers, an Adwords campaign may kick start your traffic while you are waiting for your blog to get found naturally in search results. Getting quick results like this will also allow you to see if your blog design and format is working and whether any incentives you are offering are enough to generate subscribers and leads.

- **Submit your blog to Reddit and Stumbleupon:** Both of these websites allow their users to rate web content. Reddit is a collection of webpages which have been submitted by its users. Stumbleupon is a collection of web pages that has been given the thumbs up. You can submit pages directly on its submit page or by installing the Firefox add-on or the Chrome extension. It is best not add too many of your own pages to Stumbleupon but make sure you add both the Reddit and Stumbleupon buttons to your blog so other people can.

## THE ESSENTIAL WORDPRESS PLUGINS FOR YOUR BLOG

One of the best things about WordPress for your blog is that it is easy to customize and you need little or no technical or design knowledge to create a great blog. There are a ton of plug-ins you can install to make your site even better, but there are so many it is difficult to choose which ones are really important. To help you, here are some plug-ins that are essential for your blog:

- **The Facebook comments plug-in:** Installing Facebook comments into your blog can be tricky, but with this easy to use plug-in you can easily administer and customize Facebook comments from your WordPress site. Another plug-in, **Facebook comments SEO,** will insert a Facebook comment form, Open Graph tags, and insert all Facebook comments into your WordPress database for better search engine optimization. When it comes to spammers, Facebook with Open Graph is managing to weed out spammers and trolls with great effectiveness. Facebook allows you to login with Facebook, Yahoo, and Microsoft Live.

- **Disqus comment system:** The other popular comment system Disqus replaces your WordPress comment system with comments hosted and powered by Disqus. It features threaded comments and replies, notifications and replies by email, aggregated comments and social mentions, full spam filtering, and black-and-white lists. Disqus allows you to login with Facebook, Twitter, and Google.

- **Facebook Chat:** This is great if you want to chat with your visitors in real time. When installed, Facebook Chat will display on the bottom right. This is great for supplying support on your site.

- **Broken Link Checker:** This essential plug-in scans your site and notifies you if it finds any broken links or missing images and then lets you replace the link with one that works.

- **RB Internal Links:** This plug-in assists you with internal links and cuts the risk of error pages and broken links.

- **Social Sharing Plugins:** There are numerous social sharing plugins available for WordPress. **Flare** is a simple yet eye-catching sharing bar that you can customize depending on which buttons you want to display. It helps to get you followed or 'liked' and helps get your content shared via posts, pages, and media types. The other great feature Flare has is that you can display your Flare at the top, bottom, or right of your post content. When Flare is displayed on the left and right of your posts, it follows your visitors down the page and conveniently hides when not needed. Other social sharing plug-ins include: **Floating Social Media Icon, Social Stickers,** and **Shareaholic,** to name but a few.

- **All-In-One Schema Rich Snippets:** Rich snippets are markup tags that webmasters can put in their sites in order to tell Google what type of content they have on their site so that Google can better display it in search results. It is basically a short summary of your page. Rich snippets are very interactive, let you stand out from your competition, and help with your search engine ranking. Unless you are a techie then implementing them can be tricky. However, this plug-in makes it really simple by giving you a meta box to fill in every time you create a new blog post.

- **Contact Form Plug-ins:** It is very important to make it easy for your visitors to contact you, and a form really does help with this. There are numerous plug-ins available for you to easily install, and here are a few: **Contact 7, Fast Secure Contact form, Contact form, and Contactme.**

- **Simple Pull Quote:** The Simple Pull Quote WordPpress plug-in provides an easy way for you to insert and pull quotes into your blog posts. This is great for bringing attention to important pieces of information and adding interest to a post.

- **Backup Plug-ins:** Backing up your files and database is essential. It may be that your hosting service provides this, but there are very good plug-ins that do this: Vaultpress, BackWPup, Backup buddy, and Backup.

- **Related Posts Plug-ins:** Related post plug-ins help your visitors to stay on your site by analyzing the content on your site and pulling in similar articles from your site for them to read. One of the most popular ones is **nrelate related** content which is simple to install and activate. **WordPress related posts** is another one.

- **Search Everything Plug-in:** This plug-in increases the ability of the WordPress search, and you can configure it to search for anything you choose.

- **Google Analytics Plugin:** The Google Analytics plug-in allows you to easily integrate Google Analytics using Google Analytics tracking code.

- **Google XML Sitemaps:** It is essential that the search engines can index your site and this plug-in will generate a special XML sitemap.

- **SEO Friendly images:** This plug-in automatically adds alt and title attributes to all your images, which helps to improve traffic from search engines.

- **Akismet (Comments and Spam):** The more traffic you receive, the more likely it is for you to receive spam and fake comments. Akismet checks your comments against Akismet web services to see if they look like spam or not and then lets you review it under your comments admin screen.

- **Social Author Bio:** Social Author Bio automatically adds an author box along with Gravatar and social icons on posts.

- **Thank Me Later:** This great little plug-in automatically sends a thank you note by email to anyone who has commented on your blog. You can personalize your email and set up exactly when you want to send it, and you can set it up to only send it out once or as a chain of emails. This plug-in is great for engaging people who comment on your blog, and you could use it to encourage people to join your opt-in.

## MEASURING YOUR RESULTS

Measuring the success of your blog is crucial in order to steer your blog in the right direction so that your business can benefit from all the rewards a top blog can offer. Here are a number of ways you can measure your success:

### Google Analytics

You can easily measure the number of social media shares, number of leads, subscribers, and comments on your blog. For more detailed information on your blog performance, setting up a Google Analytics account is essential and will offer you a wealth of detailed information so you can measure results, including the following:

- **The number of back links:** In the left side bar under **Standard Reports** you will find a section **Traffic Sources,** and then under **Social,** you will find **Trackbacks**. You will find here any web pages that have linked to any page of your site with the number of visits.

- **The number of visits:** Obviously this is one of the most important statistics, and you will be able to easily see how many visits you have and information about where your traffic is coming from.
- **Page views:** You will be able to see which pages are generating the most interest, and therefore, you will be able to plan more content similar to this.
- **Keywords:** You can keep track of your success with how your traffic is being generated by keywords. You will be able to see if your optimization for certain keywords are working and whether your blog is being found by keywords that you had not considered. When you identify which keywords are the most popular, you can try and work them into other blog posts.
- **Conversions:** In Google Analytics you will also be able to track conversions, which is an action on your site that is important to your business. This could be a download, sign up, or purchase. You will need to define your goals in analytics in order to track the conversion. You will be able to see conversion rates and also the value of conversions if you set a monetary value. There are detailed instructions available in Google Analytics on how to set this up, or you can employ a web developer or specialist to do it.

## Chapter Sixteen

### THE ICING ON THE CAKE

FOLLOWING ALL THE steps, instructions, and strategies is going to go a long way to making your campaign succeed, but what does it take to make you really good? If you have ever followed or are following certain brands on social media, you will probably have discovered that there are certain brands or businesses that stand out from the crowd. These are the brands and businesses that seem bigger than their products. These are the ones who usually have a sizeable and highly targeted audience, the best quality content, the greatest amount of interaction and engagement, and often post viral content. They literally have their audience hanging on their every word and get the highest open rates for their emails. They appear to understand their audience and relate to them by going out of their way by either helping them to achieve their dreams, calm their fears or confirm their suspicions, and offer them incredible value. It is obvious by the interaction that they have built a loving and respecting community, and you can be almost sure that all this is transferring to their balance sheets. These businesses are what I call 'The Social Media Superstars.' They are the game changers and they truly know how to leverage the power of social media to work for their business.

These 'Social Media Superstars' can often be compared to those party animals who always seem to be the most popular at any party and are more often than not surrounded by an audience of engaged and happy people having a great time. These people also always seem to be the most interesting, the most interested, the most charismatic, and the most engaged. They almost always tend to be good listeners as well. So how can you emulate this scenario, and what does it take to stand out from the crowd in Facebook marketing?

## It's all about your audience and a few other things!

The reasons these individuals, businesses, and brands are good at social media marketing is not because they have particular powers. It's not by chance or coincidence. It's because they know that it's all about the audience and a few other things!

Of course your aim is to ultimately benefit your business, but in order to do this you need to make it all about your audience and what they want. If you give them what they want by either making their life better or easier in some way or solving a problem they may have, then you are going to build a valuable base of fans who trust you, open your emails, and are ready to go to the next step and buy your product. You will find that your fans will become ambassadors and advocates and will then be doing the work for you by sharing your content and promoting your brand in the most powerful way, word-of-mouth. To achieve this and stand out from the crowd, you need to go the extra mile by doing the following:

- Being fully committed and positive about your campaign and in it for the long term
- Totally believing in what you are offering. This could be your product, your service, or yourself, if you are a personal brand.
- Making it all about your audience, knowing exactly who they are, what makes them tick, what they need, and how to connect with them
- Putting your audience's needs above your own and demonstrating the rich content and service you provide
- Putting the relationship with your audience first, by listening to them, understanding them, and embracing conversation where you can
- Offering your audience incredible value with free information and advice
- Being authentic and true to your brand

So if there is one piece of insight I want to leave you with, it is this:

## IT'S ALL ABOUT YOUR AUDIENCE and WHAT THEY WANT

I really hope you have enjoyed the book, have found it of great value, and that you will continue using it as your manual for your success on Facebook. The world of social media is continually changing, and it is my commitment to keep updating the books when these changes happen. If you would like to continue receiving these social media updates by email, please sign up at www.alexstearn.com

I would love your feedback about the book and would be very grateful if you could take just a moment to leave a review on Amazon at this link . By leaving a review you can also enter the Prize draw for a Kindle Fire HD at this link and of course please feel free to contact me if you have any questions at alex@alexstearn.com

I have also written a series covering all the major social media platforms including: Twitter, Google + , Pinterest, Instagram, Tumblr, YouTube and the Big Book ,Make Make Social Media Work for your Business which includes all the books, available on Amazon from $9.99 available at this link http://bit.ly/alexauthor

Lastly, I have also set up a group on Facebook called 'Make Social Media Work for your Business.' The group was created for supporting each other in our social media efforts, for networking, and also as a place for finding out about the latest social media developments. You can join at this link http://bit.ly/yourgroup

I will also be continually posting helpful and inspirational tips on my Facebook page, and look forward to connecting with you there or on any of your preferred social networks.

Make Facebook Work For Your Business

Website: www.alexstearn.com

www.facebook.com/alexandrastearn
www.instagram.com/alexstearn
www.twitter.com/alexstearncom
www.pinterest.com/alexstearn
www.alexstearn.tumblr.com
www.youtube.com/alexstearn
www.linkedin.com/in/alexstearn
www.google.com/+alexstearn

# Other Books in the Series

## Make Social Media Work for your Business
### The complete series in one book!
The complete guide to marketing your business, generating new leads, finding new customers, and building your brand on Twitter, Pinterest, LinkedIn, Instagram, Google +, Tumblr, YouTube, Facebook, Foursquare, Vine and Snapchat.

## Make Twitter Work for your Business

## Make Instagram Work for your Business

## Make Pinterest Work for your Business

## Make Google + Work for your Business

## Make YouTube Work for your Business

## Make Tumblr Work for your Business

# We'd love to hear from you

Thank you for your recent purchase of 'Make Facebook Work for your Business' I really hope you have enjoyed the book and your business will benefit greatly.

If you have any questions about the book or about social media marketing in general, please do not hesitate to contact me by email at **alex@alexstearn.com** or on **Facebook at www.facebook.com/alexandrastearn** and I will do my best to reply as soon as possible. I also offer regular updates, ebooks and social media tips in my newsletter at www.alexstearn.com and a group on Facebook which is all about supporting each other in our social media efforts and networking. Would love you to join us at this link
http://bit.ly/yourgroup

Lastly, if you have enjoyed the book I would also be so grateful if you could leave a review on Amazon, your feedback is so valuable and also helps others benefit from your experience.

Looking forward to seeing you in the group

8218183R00110

Printed in Germany
by Amazon Distribution
GmbH, Leipzig